The Maid's Tale

Rose Plummer was born in 1910 in Hoxton, one of the poorest parts of London's East End. She left school at 15 and became a live-in domestic servant in a house in the West End. For the next 15 years she saw at first hand what life below stairs was really like. She met her future husband John, a footman, just before the start of the Second World War and though there were no children they enjoyed a long and happy marriage. After the war Rose had a number of jobs, but never again in domestic service. She died in 1994.

The Maid's Tale

As told to Tom Quinn

CORONET

First published in Great Britain in 2011 by Coronet
An imprint of Hodder & Stoughton
An Hachette UK company

1

A CIP catalogue record for this title is available from the British Library

ISBN 978 1 444 73586 4
Ebook ISBN 978 1 444 73587 1

Typeset in Sabon MT by Hewer Text UK Ltd, Edinburgh

Printed and bound by CPI Group (UK), Croydon, CR0 4YY

Hodder & Stoughton policy is to use papers that are natural, renewable
and recyclable products and made from wood grown in sustainable forests.
The logging and manufacturing processes are expected to conform to the
environmental regulations of the country of origin.

Hodder & Stoughton Ltd
338 Euston Road
London NW1 3BH

www.hodder.co.uk

Acknowledgements

I'd like to thank the late Rose Plummer for letting me write her story, Mark Booth at Hodder for agreeing to publish it and Charlotte, Katy, Alex, James, Joe and Emma for ensuring I finished it on time.

Introduction

We are all fascinated by the vanished world of upstairs downstairs, a world where the wealthy led lives of unimaginable luxury, cosseted by armies of servants. Fictional representations of this world, especially on television, invariably show houses where servants and family get on reasonably well or at least have some lively, positive connection with each other. Servants bustle about in this world looking well fed and content, their lives filled with gossip about the family and each other.

Few now remember what life in service was really like, but one thing is certain: it was not the cosy world of mutual interdependence we see in fiction. It was more often than not a harsh world of long hours and low pay, where servants were owned, almost body and soul, by their employers.

Rose Plummer, whose memories are recorded in this book, knew that world at first hand and her memory of it remained undimmed into old age. I first met Rose in 1985 while researching a project on everyday life in London at the end of the Great War. After five minutes with her it became clear to me that she deserved a whole book to herself. Her natural flair for storytelling, honed in the pre-television era in which she grew up, was combined with a pin-sharp memory for the long-vanished streets of her childhood and youth in London.

A slight figure with delicate, pearl grey hair and eyes that were sometimes mischievous and sometimes fierce, Rose spent her last years in an old people's home. She was hugely popular with her fellow residents. One of her friends said, 'The thing about Rose is that she never says anything boring. She lights the room up with fun and laughter.'

This was certainly true and, remarkably, Rose seemed able to transform even the worst of her early experiences into something life enhancing. For despite the poverty of her childhood and the treatment she received when she worked as a maid in various houses in the 1920s and 1930s, she had an extraordinarily positive outlook on life. She loved the fact that she had lived from the age of horses into the age of space travel. She loved the fact that, having grown up in a slum, she was now able to live in a centrally heated room surrounded by kindness. With the memory of her own harsh treatment as a domestic servant always in mind, she was charm itself to those who now looked after her.

She regretted the passing of some aspects of the world she had known as a young woman, but she never fell into the nostalgic trap that afflicts so many accounts of the past. This, her level headedness and her good humour makes Rose's story unique and memorable.

After that first interview I saw Rose several times over the succeeding years. Despite age and increasing infirmity it was still easy to see that she had been a beauty in her youth. And if she laughed a little less towards the end she still liked to shock with her outspoken and always radical views. The last time I saw her she was looking out of her bedroom window and smiling to herself. As I left she turned and said, 'The past doesn't really matter any more, but I'm glad you wrote it all down.'

Chapter One

Hoxton was a rough old place in 1910 when I was born in the two rooms my mum and dad rented down a little back alley just off Hoxton Square. There were houses in the square from Elizabeth I's time with fancy doorways and windows. They were very grand houses I remember but long ago split up into cheap rooms and a bloody great family in each, but still.

Of course I didn't know any of this history at the time. I only really found out about it years after I'd left and done a bit of reading. Back then Hoxton was just where we lived and everyone would have thought you were mad if you talked about its history or the way the houses were built.

All the houses were smoke-blackened and damp. Many were propped up with timbers and we cursed the fact we had to live in them. But Hoxton was home and just the sort of poor place that thousands of girls who ended up in domestic service started from.

I had six brothers and sisters who lived and a few more born before me who died in infancy or were stillborn. My brother Jimmy died in the war. Bob went to America and died one terrible winter from the cold. A sister died from TB. But in a way we were lucky because when TB hit a family it often carried everyone off.

We did all the things that poor East Enders did. We shared beds and were boiled in summer and frozen in winter. But what always comes back to me is not the memory of those two drab little rooms we slept and ate in, but the streets and squares of the East End. That was where, as a child and a young girl, I really lived.

Chapter Two

Hoxton, Stepney and Mile End, Whitechapel and Bow. They'd all definitely seen better times. And people used to say about poor old Hoxton that it had more criminals than any other square mile in Britain. But it didn't really seem like that at the time because we were all in it together and everyone knew someone who did the odd bit of thieving. Thieving was a trade like any other, for some.

Hoxton was a bloody noisy area too. In fact it's the din that I remember most from the time I started to notice anything much round about. This would be about 1918 when the war had just ended and I was eight. It seems marvellous when I look back and think how I started in a world where horses and carts still went clattering up the streets. It was a world where I was at the bottom and seemed destined to scrub floors for my whole life. Yet I survived and lived on into a world where hardly anyone had servants. Then no one treated me like dirt just because I was what they used to call common. So didn't I travel a long way?

The hardest thing to describe about my childhood is the way East London looked and sounded and smelled. Carts were terribly noisy with their great big iron-shod wheels going over granite cobbles. Motorcars and lorries were only really just coming in. People were amazed by motors and talked about them in the way they later went on about bloody computers.

But those old motors were very noisy, too, and you can't

imagine the chaos of cars and horses and carts all fighting for space with each other in the narrow roads – and the wide ones come to that – down the East End before the bombs cleared us all out.

And there were loads of other noises too. There were street vendors everywhere – well, everywhere except down the little back alleys and closes where the poorest lived and sometimes even there. All the vendors were shouting their heads off, from the cat's-meat man to dolly sellers, peg sellers and the rabbit-meat man.

Everywhere in summer there seemed to be little bands of musicians, too. There were sometimes jugglers, all sorts of street entertainers – almost always, in my memory, dark and mysterious looking because they were nearly always foreign. I remember one little group had black hats and dark beards – we called them the Jew men. We weren't being nasty and they weren't probably Jews but what did we know? We couldn't understand a bloomin' word they said but we loved their music. They had a couple of fiddles, a squeezebox – I mean an accordion – and I think in reality they were probably Italians or gypsies.

But imagine what it was like for us who had no music at home – no radio, no TV, nothing? When you heard music out in the street you got out there as quick as you could and if you paid them a penny they might hang around and play a bit longer, and if they didn't then we'd follow them down to their next pitch.

I don't think people were so self conscious then – us kids, girls *and* boys, would start dancing right in front of the musicians till a bit of a crowd got round us. So they'd play their violins and accordions and we'd all have a laugh. Best of all was the hurdy-gurdy man. He had a funny looking instrument that made a lovely noise like a cross between the bagpipes and a guitar. Unless you've heard one you just can't imagine it.

Then there was the barrel organ. This wasn't played by a foreigner. It was played by an old local man and it was a two-foot-square wooden box balanced on a four-foot pole. This pole sort of leant on the old man to stop the organ toppling over. The box was polished wood with what looked like an oil painting of mountains all over one side. The old man slowly turned a handle, like a big clock key, and it played lovely tunes that made you think of a fairground. On top of the organ box there was always a sad looking little monkey dressed in a woollen suit that tried to bite you if you got too close.

I reckon the old man had been working the streets for 50 or more years. My mother remembered him from when she was young. He had a big beard but with no moustache – you saw that a lot back then – and a pork-pie hat, waistcoat and the dirtiest trousers I've ever seen. He used to say: 'I played for the old Queen, you know.' He had a little note pinned to his organ which said he'd played for their majesties Victoria and Albert at Windsor but had fallen on hard times.

I'm sure that was a load of old rubbish but it was part of his patter. Everyone in the East End had his or her patter. Patter was a story people had ready to tell anyone who would listen – it wasn't necessarily true but it wasn't bad like a lie. It was like a sales pitch, really.

I used to worry about the organ grinder's monkey. It was small and it must have got very hot in summer, in its little suit. But no one would have thought of sticking up for the monkey, because we saw animals used for all sorts of things back then. Dogs and cats just wandered around and no one really fed them. They ate what they could find or starved – like the rest of us.

That organ grinder was a big feature of my childhood. He used to curse all the time under his breath at the poor old monkey. We thought his cursing was really funny, and sometimes we were a bit wicked and we'd tease him and run away. Then he'd get very angry and shake his fist at us, but he couldn't run after us or the organ would fall over.

The organ was one more noise that added to the great endless noise of the streets. But if it was noisy it was also bright and busy, at least in summer – it wasn't always drab like those old photos you see.

I remember the brightly painted open top buses, rumbling in and out of the horses and carts. The buses were absolutely covered in advertisements and must have been bloody freezing in winter on account of there being no heating. We would have loved to go on them but you needed money for that – a penny a ride was too much for us.

Then, on a Sunday, it all went quiet because trading wasn't allowed then and this was enforced by the police. Sunday was a serious business even if, like us, you didn't bother with church. A lot of East Enders thought the church was a waste of time because it was another place where you were supposed to kowtow to the toffs or to God who seemed pretty posh to us. The problem was: if you didn't go to church, what did you do? The shops were shut and the pubs only opened at midday and in the evening. Most of the men waited for the pubs to open standing around on street corners talking to their mates.

The traffic, the street entertainers and the men outside pubs are among my earliest memories. Not a stick of that world is left. It might just as well have never existed. Mostly I'm glad it's gone. Apart from the poverty it was sometimes violent. People think there's too much violence in the modern world but it was much worse back then.

If any of my dad's mates had seen a man with his hair dyed red or blue like you see today they'd likely get shouted at and maybe punched. There were a lot more street fights then, often outside pubs, and most people didn't think much of trying to stop them. They were a bit of entertainment, so they'd even egg them on. I remember as a little girl sitting outside a pub trying to get a penny for the old Guy – it was November – when a fight broke out. It was half exciting and half terrifying, but it was all over in a few minutes. The two men suddenly made it up. As often as not the men who got into fights outside pubs were so drunk that they'd fight and then put their arms around each other and go back into the pub best of friends – then come out ten minutes later and start at each other again! Pubs and drink were central to our lives. Everyone drank and often from early in the morning. They'd have a nip at home and small children were still given a drop – gin I mean – to keep them quiet. People liked alcohol because they were suspicious of the water – 50 families often shared a tap and memories of typhoid outbreaks were always fresh in people's minds.

On a day-to-day level people were much harsher to each other. If there was a fight no one could phone the police because no one had a phone. Anyway people didn't trust the police. They wouldn't shout for a policeman if their lives depended on it.

It was only when a copper happened along, which was rare, that the fight would stop. I can even remember two women fighting. There they were in bright floral aprons punching and kicking each other in a street near us. I must have been about 12 years old at the time and my best friend and I were walking down a street just beyond Columbia Road market – all the houses have gone now – and we heard a right old racket going on. I looked up and saw a grey-haired woman looking out of an upstairs window and shouting at the top of her voice, 'Go on, fuckin' 'it her!'

She was leaning out of a tiny, crumbly little soot-blackened house with two storeys and one window in each storey and the front door right on the pavement. But the house so low that even when you looked out the top window you were only about ten feet up! She was leaning out as relaxed as you like, dirty grey hair hanging down and not a tooth in her head, shouting the odds.

There was a bit of a crowd gathered and we pushed our way through to watch. These two middle-aged women were having a terrible row in front of everyone. They didn't mind a bit that people were watching and jeering because they were so furious with each other. They tore at each other's hair and scratched and kicked and I remember noticing that the men were laughing. They only butted in to pull them apart after they'd had a good long look.

You see, there was a bit of us that liked the excitement of a fight because there wasn't much entertainment. Otherwise the women did look a bit shame-faced when they were pulled apart, but then they still tried to take a swing or two at each other even after it was all over. Some of the younger children watching were crying because they were scared. But of course they'd see their older brothers and sisters laughing and soon imitate them.

What would amaze anyone now was that these wild cats were really just two old dears. Probably in their 50s or 60s, but to me, back then, they looked like a couple of grannies. And it wasn't that rare to see women fighting then. I don't remember seeing it beyond about 1940.

But for all the fights and noise and dirt our life was on the streets and not at home, which is why I remember so much from outside and so little from those two damp rooms, except the smell of small bodies in a lumpy bed and ice on the windows on winter mornings.

When you have a lot of children in one room and they hardly ever wash they smell like mice. At the time I liked the smell! It was comforting.

Chapter Three

We had our two little rooms. I can't say I was unhappy there because there was no time to wonder if you were happy or unhappy. I would certainly be a lot more unhappy later when I went into domestic service.

We had no books or games at home except a pack of cards and so, like everyone not bed-ridden, we were out all the time. I wandered the streets with my friends from about the age of five. I don't remember my mum worrying that I'd be snatched or hit by a car. I think it was a relief for her when we were out.

My main memory of her is that she was permanently exhausted. I hardly remember ever seeing her sit down for a minute, what with trying to manage a small army of children.

That's why winters were so bloomin' awful. It was hard to go out because of the weather and there was nothing to do indoors. We sometimes wrapped up a bit and went up West to look in the shop windows which, to us, looked like something from the planet Mars. Shops in Bond Street and Piccadilly were out of this world with their gaslight and sparkle.

Older kids might walk miles to West London or out into Essex looking for odd jobs, stealing a bit here and there. Some teenage boys drifted away and were never heard of again. Some went to sea or joined the army. I remember one kid who'd have been about 16 years, made a few shillings a week catching birds. He'd walk a round trip of about 30 miles out into Essex, catch a few birds and bring them back in little wire cages he'd made himself and he'd sell them as good singers. He'd go up towards Aldgate where almost no one lives now – it's all offices – and stand about dodging the coppers and shouting 'Birds, birds, lovely singers' at the top of his voice. Sometimes he made good money, but I always felt so sorry for those birds.

I'd love to be able to bring those shops back to life. The rich had all their stuff delivered from big shops with bright lights and cut glass and pictures everywhere. The bigger shopkeepers tried to make their shops look so inviting that you just couldn't keep away – with gas lamps, big mirrors, carpets and sofas – and a man at the door to stop the poor getting in.

Poor people got chivvied a lot more then, especially by the police. When we were up West we instinctively kept a look out for the coppers, even as children. My dad used to call them the Peelers, which was a really old-fashioned word even then. Well, the Peelers knew we were East Enders, or poor kids anyway, from our clothes and they'd often move us on if we hung around too long outside a posh shop. The police were seen by poor people as there to protect the rich from us. We didn't really like the police. They were always moving us on. They'd be as rude as they liked and threaten us but they'd grovel to anyone smartly dressed. The class thing went through everything back then. That's why I liked it when all that stopped and you didn't have to look up to the toffs any more.

By the time I was in my 70s the police had to be nice to us!

But in the 1920s there was none of that 'everyone is equal' business, because we weren't bloody equal, were we? I knew that when I was a kid and it would be knocked even further into me when I became a maid.

In the West End you'd see coppers on the beat everywhere, but in the East End there were far fewer, because there wasn't much property to defend. We didn't have much, anyway, and they never really felt safe there. And poor people stealing from other poor people, which happened all the time, wasn't seen as a problem. Ordinary people like us were assumed to have been born too stupid to know right from wrong. It never occurred to anyone that we might just be ignorant because our parents couldn't afford to send us to Eton. The well off thought the poor were born stupid and criminal. 'It's bred in them' was what they used to say.

Later on when I got a bit more militant I used to tell my friends that the aristocracy were born speaking Latin and Greek. They didn't have to learn it because it was bred in them. We were always taking the mickey when I was a girl – which made it difficult when I went into service, as you'll see, because you had to mind your lip there or lose your job.

So on winter days, if we wanted to get out of those two rooms and didn't go up West, we might walk down to the river near the docks or just play in the street. If you went down to the docks you'd get lost in about five minutes. In the 1920s they went for miles, and the lanes and alleys round about them were a jumble of cranes and carts and gantries, especially around the Old Pool – that's what they called the bit below Tower Bridge where all the ships were laid up side by side.

We loved looking at the ships because they came from all over the world. You could only see them from the bridge. It was hard to get into the docks themselves, as they were so closely guarded. The owners were always worried stuff would get nicked. Of course it did get nicked and by the ton because with tens of thousands of dockers going in and out you couldn't police it.

At low tide we used to watch the kids looking for anything valuable in the mud along the river's edge. These were mudlarks raking for any old bits and pieces. They weren't after ancient bits of silver and coins, just after stuff that had fallen off the ships, but I wonder how much archaeological stuff disappeared after they picked it up?

All the metal they found they'd sell to the scrap metal dealers or the totters – the rag-and-bone men who went round collecting. They were called rag-and-bone men, but they really wanted metal. I think the rags went into paper and the bones were used by the glue makers.

Only a few years before my time kids still collected dog shit to sell to the leather tanners. I think it stopped because they found a chemical that would do the job better. There were loads of jobs back then that no one does now. Dockers have all gone along with the rag-and-bone men.

We also knew people who used to go down the sewers looking for lost jewellery, and coins, but that was dying out by the 1920s. Apart from being a really dirty job, it was dangerous because of the build up of gas. And there were rats, rats as big as a Jack Russell. People told stories about how generations of families worked the sewers in the old days and became immune to all the filth and disease.

The streets were always fun, but now and then, very occasionally, we had other entertainments.

There was the Hackney Empire Music Hall and a smaller music hall on Islington Green. You could go in the cheap seats up in the gods for a few pennies, but even the cheap seats were too much for us. I did go once, but none of the famous stars who performed there were on that night. Marie Lloyd used to perform now and then, and Stan Laurel, but what I remember was the music and the laughter.

The audience wasn't quiet and respectable. If they didn't like an act they'd boo and hiss and if they were bored they'd just talk to each other as if they were out on the street.

When I was a girl the Hackney Empire was still quite new. It had been built around the turn of the century, about 1901 I think. It was a marvel with its gaslights and all the plush velvet and golden cherubs all over the place. It was like a palace to me who had never been anywhere.

The evening I went they had several singers. One pretended

to be a chimney sweep, the other a toff. They had a juggler and a contortionist but most of the fun was just being there in the bright lights and talking and shouting your head off.

When you don't have money or toys and there's a bunch of you, you'd be amazed how the day still passes and you can have a lovely time just making things up and talking. We used to talk for bloody hours. But we also liked anything new. When everything around you is old and there are very few novelties you grab any little novelty that comes along.

I remember when a bloke we knew down the road got himself a wireless. When there was a broadcast, we used to hang around at his door the whole time asking to be let in, but he didn't often say yes. He was fed up of being pestered I should think. Having a radio so soon after the First World War it made you a celebrity. The few times us kids were allowed in to listen reminded me of going into church. This was because his house was a bit bigger than most round us and a lot older too. It had been a boarding house and then been let out as rooms. I remember it had a great big fancy fireplace in the hall all carved and the hall was wide with a high ceiling. It had a massive old staircase that was all crooked and a thick banister you could slide down. We'd go up the stairs really quiet in case he changed his mind. We'd go in his little parlour, which seemed to me to be full of junk. Then we'd take turns listening through these funny headphones he had. He'd let you listen for about 20 seconds each and then tell us to get out. He was grumpy, but I think he was kind-hearted too. His name was Power and I think that like a lot of East Enders he was Irish. All the histories of East London mention the Jews. Few mention the Irish but there were tens of thousands of them and they were a very nice set of people in the main. There were also a few Indians, although they mostly stayed down towards Shoreditch and worked in the docks.

I don't know what old Power did for a living, but I heard later, when I was a good bit older, that he knew the Krays. Valence Road, where the Krays grew up, wasn't far from us. I think it's a load of old nonsense when people said everyone loved the Krays. They were really rough even by the standards of the East End and people only liked them when they got rich and powerful in the 1960s. You had to like them then or they'd come round and sort you out.

So there were the the Irish and the Indians, but also quite a few Chinese and what we called Lascars – I think they were some kind of Indians. As kids we were bloody terrified of all of them, except the Irish. My mum used to say that if we didn't behave they would come and get us and take us to Africa. I think she had a vague idea that India and Africa were more or less the same place!

Chapter Four

A lot of the backstreets and alleyways still had cobbles before the war. They only got properly surfaced with tarmac much later. My uncle worked in some parts of London where they found wooden blocks that had been used, end-upwards to make the roadway. But most of what we knew was endless houses and streets of Victorian shops cobbled with all their goods laid out on the footpath in front of them.

Meat was always left outside the butchers' shops, hanging in the air right through the long summer day. It's amazing we weren't all poisoned. In those days they couldn't advertise much, which is why they made the front of the shop an advertisement. You should have seen the front of the poulterers' shops in the city in winter – it was as good as a play. From the ground to about 20 feet up there would be rows of pigs, rabbits in the skin, pheasants, hares, and pigs' heads – everything you can imagine.

Small shops down in Whitechapel, Hoxton and Shoreditch and down all the alleys and little streets in-between only sold stuff to the poor and the shopkeepers were often just as poor or nearly so themselves. They'd be dark tiny little dens where you had to ask for everything – you wouldn't help yourself to a thing or the shopkeeper would clout you because he'd assume you were about to steal it!

In the grocer's you'd ask for your potatoes and cabbage and they'd weigh them on an old set of black weighing scales where they put the vegetables in one end and then adjusted a little pile of weights on the other till it balanced at a pound or a quarter pound or whatever. A lot of the old ladies would say to the shopkeeper: 'Oi, keep yer thumb off!' meaning, 'Don't cheat me.' The trick was to set up the scales so that one end was hidden by something on the counter and then the shopkeeper could push that end down a little so you thought you were getting a pound of whatever where you were actually getting just 12 ounces.

The little shops were incredibly dingy places and by today's standards most were very unhygienic, with stuff kept on the shelves for ages. As well as being small the shops sold really small quantities – people often bought one or two potatoes and a carrot or they'd buy one cigarette. The shopkeeper made a bit more that way because a packet of ten cigarettes bought one at a time would cost more than ten bought together. The shop-keepers also gave credit to people they knew and this often caused a lot of bitter feeling when people failed to pay their debts, which happened often through no fault of their own.

The shopkeepers used to vie with each other, because the bigger and better your shop front the more likely it was you'd get the customers. It used to take about two hours to open the shop and get the front ready each day. And in parts of the East End there would be violin shops next to German beer shops next to Jewish tailoring and jewellery and boot repair busi-nesses. There were Jewish businesses all over the East End. They kept themselves to themselves, though, and people were sometimes rude to them, I'm sorry to say. People used the word 'Jewish' to mean tight-fisted. I know it wasn't very nice, but it was sort of automatic and in many ways we weren't very nice. It was a tough world, harsh and cruel in lots of ways, as I try to explain.

All this time I was growing up I never thought I'd be a maid or work in service. My mum never talked about it and no one in the family had gone into service before, but I should have known it was a possibility. It was either that or work in a factory or take in a bit of mending or washing, which was the worst paid of the lot, and you could hardly get that kind of work where we were. We lived too far from anyone who could afford to get their washing done by someone else! But of course all the jobs I saw people doing around me were skivvy jobs really – delivery boys, shop assistants, milkmen, the butcher, the coalman. Labour was cheap and we were the cheap labour.

I remember mile after mile of tall narrow buildings all with tiny shops at the front. They mostly disappeared with the bombing or were knocked down after the war. They were bloody drab and really knocked about. People probably thought the sooner they were knocked down the better as they were full of vermin. Later on the few that survived the bombs were restored and turned into millionaires' houses.

When I look back I am a bit ashamed about how little my family knew London, despite the fact we lived there and went about like anyone else. The problem was we never really left the bit where we lived for long. We might go down Valence Road and beyond to the Whitechapel Road, and we occasionally walked down the West End as I've said, or to the Tower of London. But that was about it and even those little outings were rare. On a Sunday we did go now and then to see the escapologists and fire and sword swallowers – on Tower Hill. We never went in the Tower of London itself. That was for the posh kids with money.

The main thing about London and the East End in particular back then was that all the houses looked roughly the same. You might get a street where there were one or two slightly bigger houses in a terrace of small houses and maybe a really big house on the corner. Other terraces were made up of what had probably once been a big old house that had had new houses added to it on either side in the nineteenth century. But to us they were all just old. The other thing is that they were all the same colour. If they were red or yellow brick there was no way to tell because every inch of the outside walls and windows had about a hundred years' worth of soot all over it. Very rarely someone would paint the outside – usually the window frames. Then the house stuck out a mile but only for a bit. A few winter smogs and it would revert to the old smoke-blackened colour. And of course a lot of those buildings hadn't had any repair work or maintenance for decades. They were owned by landlords who charged cheap rents and had no intention of wasting money smartening up their houses for the likes of us.

There were a few new blocks of flats, but none of the concrete ones they later put up all over the place, turning the East End into an even bigger slum than ever. There were the old Peabody flats just off Kingsland Road and others like them. They seemed like luxury to us, because the people who lived in them had indoor toilets.

Our little houses all had shared toilets out the back. Sometimes a hundred families would share one or two toilets, and they were never cleaned. If they hadn't been outside where the air could get at them no one could have gone in because the smell was bad enough as it was. The floor would be a terrible mess and people only had newspaper to use. There were no loo rolls back then or if there were we didn't know about them. I can remember queuing for bloody ages to go to the loo and then it was a horrible experience. It was easier for the men who'd nip down an alley or over a wall sometimes rather than wait. But a lot of women still wore very long skirts, so when they went to the toilet it was tricky not to get the bottoms of your skirt soaked with muck. I used to take a bit of newspaper with me to put on the loo and then I'd sit on that!

Our two rooms weren't much to write home about. One room had a bed in it and a table – a big square Victorian thing with massive legs. Here we ate, mum mended and we sat when we weren't running around outside. Mum and Dad slept in the bed in this room. We had a few chairs and a much bigger bed in the other room where us kids slept under a ton of blankets. There were no sheets. When they were older the boys slept on a mattress on the floor behind a curtain pulled half way across the room. It sounds awful, but it wasn't really because at the time we knew no different. You always think what you grow up with is normal. We mostly slept in our clothes in winter because it was so cold and in a shirt in summer.

If ever you could, you got out in the morning and played or went about with your friends till nightfall. I say 'if ever you could' because I had to help my mum with various things from when I was about five – nip down to the shop, look after the fire, clean the floor, that kind of thing.

On winter mornings I can remember snuggling up to my sister for warmth. I must have been three or four and there were four of us in that bed.

The mattress was filled with lumpy straw. It was also full of bedbugs and even spiders.

Our two rooms may not sound much but they gave us more space than many people had. Sometimes lots of families lived in one room.

There were oil lamps and a coal fire when it was really cold. When we ran out of oil we used candles, although these cheap candles were horrible and smoky. I think there was a lot of animal fat in them. We bought the coal by the bucketful unless we suddenly had a bit of money, in which case we bought a sack and had it delivered.

We didn't know much at all about hygiene or washing. People thought it was bad for you to change your clothes too much. Most people would have a bath about once a month at most and then it was only a bit of an all-over splash with cold or tepid water. After the age of about 50 a lot of people stopped washing completely, especially old ladies. They were too exhausted to bring in a tin bath and boil loads of kettles. There was also the risk anyway of catching cold by taking your clothes off. The truth is we were all really smelly. When you are poor, washing is a luxury you can't really afford. No one had heard of deodorant. And I never saw deodorant until the 1960s. It didn't exist. Some people of course did wash a lot, often down at the municipal baths, but not the really poor, the out-of-work or those with big families. How could they? They had no time and could only just afford to keep the family in food let alone pay tuppence for each of them to have a bath once a week.

I knew one family where the children were sewn into their winter clothes in November and not taken out again until the following March. Other parents used to plaster their kids with lard or goose fat and then put them in their clothes for three months. The fat kept the heat in and the germs out, they used to say. They thought that was the best way to stop them catching cold or the dreaded TB. If a child started coughing people didn't automatically assume it was TB because we had colds and flu all the time, but TB was always a possibility and whole families got carried off with it. Only the tough survived.

Chapter Five

So there we were. Unwashed, barely housed and left to run about the streets. But that's not the whole story of my childhood. It makes it sound as if no one cared what I did, which isn't true. I was one of the really lucky ones because I went to school. My mum was strict about that. I went to the local board school which looked like a bloody old workhouse to me. All tall steep gables in red brick and stone steps. It was one of those schools built specially for poor kids in the 1880s. You can still see them all over London although mine isn't there any more. There was one entrance for the girls and one for the boys and they kept us apart all day. Above the entrance, in the stone lintel, the word 'Girls' was carved – and you were in a lot of trouble if you went in the wrong gate, even as a joke.

I went to school when I was five or just about six. I seem to remember that it was only shortly after that that you were allowed to go to school without paying. I think you'd had to pay about sixpence a week only, we wouldn't have been able to pay that. My mum and dad had never been to school, so they didn't think much about sending us until someone said to my mum that we'd be able to get a better job if we could read and write a bit. So off we went. Of course we hated the idea of going, but it got us out of mischief and, looking back, I realise how lucky I was that my mum and dad ignored all my complaints about going. Most of my friends grew up almost illiterate. Some were completely illiterate.

Like all kids we wanted to run around and play and keep doing what we'd always done, but I was also curious about what school might be like. You could play anywhere you liked back then. Down our alleyway you were more likely to see a ghost than a car. But one cold autumn morning I left most of my friends playing in the alleyways and set off for school. I'm sure everyone remembers their first day at school. Even though most people would have said I was tough little urchin with a bit of a foul mouth, I couldn't help crying. It wasn't that I was sad. It was the fact that I was sent off on my own when I'd hardly ever been on my own for even a minute before that. You always went around with your mates. So I was down in the dumps and was also ashamed of my boots, which didn't fit, and an old dress I had to wear that was in a bit of a state with patches and a few rips.

We queued up outside the entrance and a woman came out and told us to be quiet and line up and then we were marched in. I can remember going up a stone staircase which seemed huge to me, although when I went back later when I was in my teens it seemed tiny. But that's probably the same for everyone.

Up the stairs we went and then into a hall where the head-master – I think it was the headmaster – spoke to us. I can honestly say I didn't really understand a word he said. We all had really strong cockney accents and he didn't. We were baffled. It was a bit like when I later went into service. The first people I worked for must have thought I was really thick because for months I often didn't understand what they were asking me to do. The East End accent was a lot stronger three-quarters of a century ago and in some ways it wasn't just an accent. The East End had its own language. It wasn't all that nonsense about cockney rhyming slang, although there was a lot of that. There was coster talk which was different from cockney or rhyming slang and even ordinary cockney wasn't what I used to hear on the telly. It was much stronger. There were lots of words that disappeared as the years went on and new people moved into the East End. We called change – meaning a handful of coins – smash, for example.

It still amazes me how our teachers and then later our employers thought we were stupid because we didn't understand posh words and accents. Looked at another way they didn't think *they* were stupid because they didn't understand us. I thought our headmaster was a foreigner when I first heard him speak!

And the other teachers were the same. I suspect they were do-gooders, hoping to make us respectable. I say that because, at different times, lots of posh types came down to the East End to try to save our souls. They weren't so worried about our bodies, unless we tried to have too much fun with them. Now, that really wasn't allowed.

These were religious types who thought that if we went to church regularly we'd work hard and stop going to the pubs and drinking and smoking and having sex outside marriage. They never got very far with that kind of thing. Everyone saw them as interfering busybodies who wanted us to stop having any fun at all. But amid all the dislike of the posh and the well-to-do, East Enders wouldn't hear a word against the most aristocratic family of the lot: the Royals. Later on, when I was a lot older and became a bit of a communist, if anyone said how they thought that prince or this princess was great and a real charmer I could never resist saying 'But they're not even British – they're all bloody Germans!'

So there I was at school. A dopey looking girl who hadn't a clue what was going on. But I needn't have worried because a lot of the other kids were far worse than me. None of the boys had socks on and a few didn't even have any shoes. I think there were about 40 children in the class and the mistress was very strict. We did everything by rote. We wrote our letters, as practice writing used to be called, for an hour, repeating the same letters again and again till we knew them by heart. Then we'd be made to read from the Bible, and then we'd do sums and a bit of geography.

I think they wanted us to know all about the British Empire in case we became miners in Africa or something. We used slates and chalk, a lot cheaper than paper and pencil, but they worked well and I quickly got the hang of it. I remember showing my mum how quickly I could write and she gave me a funny, sad look. That was one of the few times when she wasn't bustling about being practical and knocking us into shape. Years later I realised that sad look was because she was proud of me and ashamed that she couldn't read or write herself.

We were the first generation of poor Londoners who got a bit of free education. Only a bit, mind you, because loads of kids came for a few weeks or a year and then were never seen again.

So don't let anyone tell you that we all went to school till we were 12 because it's not true. Some parents were a bit worried that what we called the school board man would come round and make trouble if their kids didn't go to school, but most would just pretend they didn't have any kids when he came round. Or they'd all hide under the bed till he went away. Or they'd just tell him to fuck off — and he'd know that it wasn't worth pursuing it.

I did really well at school and only got a few smacks on the head for not paying attention. Other kids got walloped in a way they'd never get away with now. The boys were regularly caned in front of the class or even the whole school. No one would dream of answering the teacher back and the canings were usually for hopping the wag, as we used to call it — bunking off school — or for stealing or lying. Some of us were really good at all three of these! Several boys made a point of not crying when they were caned to show how tough they were, but they would never openly defy the teachers the way they do now, except by not coming to school at all. There was a boy called Toot who got the cane for being cheeky and then never came to school again. He was dragged in a few times after he'd been away for a bit but by lunchtime he'd be over the wall and away.

We were mostly still afraid of authority, I think, and slightly in awe of our betters, the teachers and so on, but it was a funny mix. Most of the time we never thought about the rich and well educated, because we neither saw nor heard anything about them. Most of us ordinary Londoners would also put on a show of being servile if we did meet someone well dressed or obviously from the respectable classes, but it was usually only in the hope of getting something out of them.

Apart from reading and writing, the other thing we did a lot of at school was sewing and mending – even ironing. Because we were girls of course, but also because the school board knew that not only were we expected to do all the domestic stuff when we got married, we were also expected – a lot of us – to end up as servants.

As well as being little toughs we were right little conservatives – really patriotic. Later on I used to think why the bloody hell *were* we so loyal? What did the people who ran the country ever do for us? In the First World War, German shops in the East End were sometimes smashed up by the mob, but no one ever said, 'Why are we doing this when even our own bloody royal family is German?' I read later that they had to change their name from Battenburg to Windsor. But what a farce was that – millions of young men going off to get killed in France because the British government and the German government wanted to find out who was top dog. And there we were, the poor of the East End, doing their dirty work for them.

Lots of East Enders died in the Great War. For the royal family it meant a few years not talking to their relatives!

If I'd said that when I was young I would probably have got a kicking, but when I looked back years later it used to make me so mad to think of the waste. Mind you, there were lots of sensible East Enders who just hid under the stairs till it was all over to avoid being called up. That's what I liked about the East

End. We might have been loyal to the royal family, but if a man decided he wasn't going to fight, his family would back him. In middle-class areas you had all that stuff with white feathers being given to men not in uniform, but there wasn't much of it down our way. There were quite a few dodgers. It was the same in the Second War – the most famous example being the Krays' dad. He didn't want to fight so he just didn't, and he kept out of the way of the police. He was a crafty one, and none of his mates would have thought any the less of him.

In the later years school became good fun. I made new friends and still had plenty of time to play. Some of my friends' dads worked down at the docks so that's where some of the boys would go when they left, although by the late 1920s there was terrible unemployment and lots of kids would have nothing to go to when school was over. In some ways, as it turned out, it was easier for girls because so many could at least get work in domestic service.

So there I was at school with no idea I would have to go into service when I left. We kids never talked about what we were going to do. We just lived day to day like all kids. I had a vague idea I might do washing or earn a few bob watching kids or get a job in a laundry or factory.

There were lots of laundry jobs in various places if you were prepared to travel a bit, but it was terrible work. Without gloves the heavy soap split your nails till they bled and most girls suffered horribly from whitlows. I knew several girls who did laundry work and hated it, but once they'd started, it was hard to get into anything else.

There were also factories that made mattresses and others that made matches – including the famous Bryant and May factory in Bow that was still there in the 1960s, I believe. But all these jobs paid a tiny amount for 12- and 14-hour days.

The Depression made people more desperate and in some ways nastier. People had a go at the Jews because they thought the Jews had it easy, which was rubbish. There were just as many poor Jews as poor Irish or cockneys. My mum had a couple of friends who were Jews. They'd been kind to her and she was bloody furious when they got blamed for things.

Hoxton was poor enough, God knows, before the Depression but it got much worse in the late 1920s and 1930s. The real Jew-hating didn't start till the 1930s when that idiot Mosley tried to get the East End on his side.

Chapter Six

Food. Mostly we thought about food. We always seemed to be hungry. Not starving but definitely hungry. People shopped for food pretty much every day. If you were out of work you got a bit of dole – a tiny amount – and you could get soup from the Salvation Army halls, but only if you sat through about two hours of bloody sermons and singing. They never fed you first – always afterwards. Cheeky buggers.

People were sometimes very kind but they could be heartless bastards too. If you were really poor and had to buy the cheapest cuts of meat everyone knew because you stood in the butchers and had to ask for what you wanted, which meant everyone else heard what you were asking for. We would feel ashamed.

We ate all sorts of things people wouldn't touch today. Everyone had liver and hearts for example. One bullock heart would feed a family for several days although, of course, without a fridge it would be a bit high by the time you finished it! Offal was cheaper then, partly because the Jews wouldn't eat it and so there was a lot of it around.

We also used to get stale bread from shops. They'd give you a big bag of it for a few pennies and it wasn't too bad if you soaked it before you ate it.

Milk came on a cart and you went out with your can and the milkman filled it up. You had to have it fresh every day, especially in summer as it went off so fast.

Much of the coal and the milk were still delivered by horse

when I was a little girl. If you went down to the River Lee or the Thames you'd see barges pulled by horses. There were also Thames sailing boats. They were called wherries. They carried cargo up and down the river. We loved to see them but they were all gone by the time the Second World War came along. Amazing they lasted that long.

One of my uncles worked on one of these boats. He was just 14 when he got a job as third hand on an old sailing barge known as an ironside to the bargees. Towards the end of my time in domestic service he used to sail to Colchester to collect sand, and he knew the Second War was coming because the sand his wherry carried was being made into millions of sandbags. He was told to keep quiet about it or face the sack.

Ned spent long periods away from home working on the barge and though the pay was poor he used to tell us that at least he'd seen the world – well compared to us he had. He'd been to Kent, Essex and Suffolk! And if the wind happened to be blowing in the wrong direction he would often get stuck for days or he'd get blown across the Channel. To us kids he was a real adventurer.

Chapter Seven

I was really lucky because I stayed at school till I was 13 years old. I left because my mum needed me and I was big enough to be a real help by then. I knew I'd have to get a job away from home eventually but what with running errands and doing a few odd jobs for a penny here and a penny there, I was 14 before it was finally decided that the best thing for me was domestic service.

The main reason I had to leave school was that my dad became really ill. He was a lovely man. A real soft heart. He was a window cleaner when he could get work, which wasn't that often. He loved jokes and mucking about. But he earned very little and before he died – he knew he was dying months before it happened – he used to say he was glad he didn't have to worry now about having no money when he was old because he never would be old.

Then he died. He was about 55, I think. We didn't really know exactly how old he was and I'm not even sure he really knew! People in the East End when he was born didn't like registering the births. They hated the authorities then and thought it would attract busybodies.

I don't think families were close then in the way that some people today say they used to be. Middle-class families probably were, because they could afford to be. How could we be close? Dad was a laugh but he didn't cuddle us much. We were all exhausted all the time and living in a couple of rooms like we did, we struggled to get any attention from our parents and they were too tired all the time and worried about making ends meet.

Dads were almost always hard on their kids. All the other kids loved my dad because he wasn't too hard. But most dads thought hitting their kids was a good idea and maybe many did it because it made them feel better about themselves and their lives.

Even really young girls had to put up with being walloped and with other sorts of pestering too. I knew a girl who was 15 when she was raped. In those days rape wasn't reported much and girls accepted it. I know that's hard to believe but they really did. If you got raped there was a feeling that you'd probably brought it on yourself in some way. Some girls even used to boast that their boyfriends knocked them about a bit. I suppose they thought it made their boyfriends sound tough, which was a big thing back then.

No one thought boys should be gentle. Where would that get them? If a girl went out and met a boy at the music hall or a dance and went off with him and then things got out of hand and he forced her, she'd just accept it afterwards. If she was knocked about a bit while he was doing it, her brothers might find the lad and give him a beating, but the Old Bill was never brought in to it. They were seen as the enemy.

Poverty was the worst thing. Worse than the odd bit of violence. Normally people don't realise working people in the 1920s and 1930s usually only had one set of clothes – they might have a couple of shirts if they were lucky and a change of underwear, but that was it. And with no dry cleaners you wore your outer skirt or trousers and you never washed them. You might sponge them down a bit, but otherwise you wore them till they fell apart. Your knickers got changed or washed at night and back on in the morning. Some girls went for a week or more without washing their underclothes and lots didn't have any underclothes at all.

A lot of the women in the East End we knew would pawn their husband's suit on a Monday and redeem it on payday – the

Friday. In the early 1930s during the Depression they'd pawn sheets and pillowcases too – I heard of people trying in desperation to pawn their underwear but the pawnbroker wouldn't take them. Imagine the humiliation!

It was all about humiliation, then. Like when my dad stopped getting work I once had to push a load of coal home in an old pram. Another time I went to the soup kitchen and brought home bacon and pea soup in an old tin tub we used for washing clothes. I had to walk half a mile carrying that with the soup getting cold and sloppin' about all over me and everyone watching. You see they knew we were broke, because I was a walking ad for the soup kitchen.

If anyone had come into that little room where I grew up and seen any of us they'd have thought what a thin lot we were. I don't remember seeing anyone who was fat till I started work in the West End. If you look at any clothes from the 1920s or 1930s in museums you'll see what I mean – tiny little bodices, cramped little jackets. We thought it was terrible back then to be thin and that no one would ever want to marry us girls because we had stick legs and scrawny faces. We were also short arses. Everyone says being short is genetic, but I think it was because we didn't get enough to eat.

The other thing about the East End and I dare say lots of other poor places was that many children had rickets. Some kids round where we lived had it really badly, because their parents kept them indoors almost all the time so they didn't get any sunlight. No one knew about vitamin D and sunlight then. I remember one boy – Johnny, that was the little lad's name – was in a terrible state: he could hardly walk he was so bow legged. But his parents never thought of going to a doctor. It would have cost too much.

Many kids were allowed to go all over the place all day, every day. I used to think maybe their parents would have been delighted if they'd never come back at all.

There was no real contraception, so people didn't choose how many kids they had. They just kept having them and a lot of husbands hated it when the woman got pregnant again and again. They'd have rows. They'd come to blows and I reckon a lot of men thought if they belted their wives they might lose the baby.

So with all that going on it's no wonder a lot of kids were neglected or shoo-ed out of the house as often as possible. Their parents just couldn't stand so many kids being around. A lot died as babies and toddlers because by modern standards they were neglected. I can remember seeing toddlers walking along the alley behind our house all on their own in just a shirt, playing in the dirt and covered in their own shit. They didn't have nappies and just wandered around poking about in the gutters. A lot of them were breast-fed till they were three or four because it was a free way to feed them.

I don't think it was always deliberate neglect. It was just that they couldn't do any more. They were exhausted and desperate, and that sometimes meant children ended up fending for themselves.

A mother with five or six kids, if she was any good, would be up at five o'clock sewing or washing at home to make a few shillings. She'd be up that early because once the children were up she had no time for herself. Maybe the kids would wake at seven or eight in the morning. Then she'd feed them and change the baby. Breakfast might be watered down milk or just water, bread and butter at the start of the week and bread and dripping towards the end. No cereals or sausages except for the better off, although we had sausages now and then, at Christmas for example. When the kids went to school a mother might get back to her sewing if the baby was sleeping or she'd start cleaning the house or the room if that was all they had.

One of the most shocking things I saw as a child was a dead baby hidden down an area at the front of an old house. The 'area' is what we called the bit below street level and just in front of of the basement windows. I'd passed this particular house loads of times and it always seemed to be semi derelict – worse even than the average, which was pretty bad. I can remember big chunks of the plasterwork areas of the brick front had fallen off and the walls were absolutely black with soot. It probably hadn't been cleaned or painted for 50 years. Anyway, I kept my eyes peeled constantly because the sharp-eyed always picked up odd pennies that had been dropped and sometimes even a three-penny bit, or a bit of jewellery or a packet of cigarettes. Anyway I saw a small white leg sticking out of the area railings and half buried in all the rubbish that had built up, so I thought 'It's a doll!' I must have been about ten. I reached down and pulled and didn't think anything of the fact that the leg felt so cold. I knew about china dolls and thought it's cold because everywhere and everything round here is cold. But as I pulled it out I realised it was a real dead baby. All down one side of its face and body it was purplish blue. The only other thing I can remember was that its stomach had swollen horribly. I didn't scream or shout or anything. I just let go, stood up and carried on walking. I was a bit surprised, but not much more. We saw shocking things all the time and you saw a lot more dead people or nearly dead people back then. Tramps were regularly found frozen to death in winter and old people often died when they caught cold and it turned into pneumonia.

In fact pneumonia was called 'the old man's friend' in those days, because it was quick. There were no antibiotics and most of the sort of medicines we could afford were useless.

Chapter Eight

My dad didn't want me to go into domestic service. He used to say: 'I don't want my girl skivvying for a load of lazy bastards unless they pay her the right amount and no one could afford the right amount not even the king or queen.' He was a nice man who always tried to make you feel good about yourself. But once he was dead it was work or starve, so just after my fifteenth birthday I was told that I had to start.

I can remember waking up at home and thinking I didn't want to get up out of the warm bed. We had a few old coats piled on top of three or four old blankets, but what really kept you warm were the other bodies. My mum came in and said, 'Come on Rose, look sharp.' I could tell she was a bit nervy and that made me worry straight away.

Then something really odd happened. I always thought of myself as a tough little girl, always ready for a laugh and rarely upset by anything; but suddenly – and I was more surprised than my mum even – I started to cry. I really felt overwhelmed. Mum brought me a big piece of bread and lard with a bit of salt on it. That was a real treat, but I knew it meant everything was about to change forever. And as I always woke up hungry the bread and dripping, as we used to call it, was delicious and it was hard to feel very sad when you felt nice and full. I can remember standing eating it at the grimy window and noticing it was starting to get light over the rooftops, which made me feel a bit better.

* * *

Anyway there I was, staring out the window and standing up in the clothes I'd slept in. It was too cold to take your clothes off for bed at that time of year and we never had pyjamas or anything like that. My mum came back in with her hat on and her coat. It was time to go.

I knew I wasn't just off for the day. I was soon going to be gone for good. I was leaving the tiny house and the cramped little streets and alleyways that I'd always known, because I was going to 'live in', as most servants did in those days.

I had no idea what to expect in this, my first job, but my mum had told me that I should just do everything I was told and not answer back or question anything ever. It wasn't that my mum was a pushover or all meek and mild. She just didn't want me to lose the job after five minutes.

She said the people I'd be working for would probably put me to sweeping and peeling vegetables, but I later realised, looking back, that she probably had no idea as she'd never been in service in a big house. She was trying to help, but bless her, she only knew the backstreets of the East End and I might just as well have been asking a lamppost as ask her.

When you know a lot of things it's very hard to imagine what it's like to know very little. I remember when I was much older and started to be interested a bit in politics someone told me to read George Orwell's *Down and Out in London and Paris*. It was a revelation to me. I had never imagined that a famous writer would bother to write about the very poorest. I loved that book but I remember he recalls meeting someone who had no idea whether Jesus was born before or after Napoleon. Well, where I was brought up I doubt if one in five would have been able to answer that question. As I say, a lot of people we knew were completely or almost completely illiterate. An old man or an old woman would sometimes come up to me in the street or in a shop and ask me to read something for them. I remember almost crying when an elderly man who seemed to have a lot of dignity about him – he had a dark little suit, a shirt and a tie, even though his clothes and face were dirty – he came up to me in a shop and asked if I could read what it said on a pot of jam. I've never forgotten him. Despite the fact that he could neither read nor write there was something special about him and he thanked me for my help with a politeness rarely heard in Hoxton.

Getting from Hoxton to the West End on that first morning wasn't too bad although, as I say, I was nervous. I reckon we could have walked to the house, which was behind where Selfridges is now, in a couple of hours, but for the first part of the journey Mum and me hopped on the back of a dray – a horse-drawn flatbed cart. No one really minded if you did this as long as you shouted up to the driver first, and my mum was a bit of a charmer so they never said no.

So we sat on the dray and looked back as the East End receded and we headed toward Kingsland Road, the main north–south road out of the City. While we were rumbling along I started thinking about the job. I realised that I never really knew how my mum even got me the job in the first place.

But parents then didn't tend to discuss things with their kids. You just got told what to do. She wouldn't have answered an advertisement in the paper. She wouldn't have known how. So it was probably by word of mouth, which is how most things happened back then, especially jobs. It would probably have filtered through the servant grapevine.

Soon we swung into the Kingsland Road. We hopped off our dray and hopped on another cart going down towards the City. I can remember looking round and thinking I might have enough money to get a bus one of these days now I'll be earning.

That was exciting for me, as a bus filled with very smartly dressed people passed us going the other way. Buses all looked like they were full of cloth at that time because women's skirts were still long and the better off the woman the more skirts she seemed to wear. And their hats were bloody enormous!

The traffic was terrible, especially as we got nearer the City. Though people were supposed to drive on the left a lot of the streets hadn't been widened yet – they did most of the widening after the Second War – so there were snarl-ups and bottlenecks everywhere. And when you add to that the fact that cars and motor lorries were mixed up with horse-drawn traffic, it was a right bloody din.

There was horse shit still on the roads, too, and that journey to my job was one of the last times I saw someone running about collecting it in a bag. I spotted him as we turned into Old Street and jumped off the cart. He would have made a few pence for each bag as it was good for people's roses. His was a trade that wasn't going to last long as carts were disappearing fast. In fact the speed with which the cars and motor lorries took over was amazing. You'd see tip-up carts and delivery vans and drays dumped up alleyways and backstreets more and more as people shifted away from them and left them to rot.

Old Street, which runs into Pentonville Road when it reaches the Angel, Islington, was reasonably smart in those days. The houses all along were much bigger than we were used to, but no less soot-blackened than anywhere else. There were a lot more cars here, too. Horses lasted longer in poor areas such as the East End. In fact a lot of East Enders still had their milk delivered by horse and cart in the 1950s.

People talk to me about when there was still horse transport as if it was a golden age, but no one thought that in the 1920s. Cars were like magic and everyone wanted one. People hated everything to do with the past, especially poor people, who walked everywhere and lived in cramped little houses. I laugh when people are nostalgic about those days. I've read stuff about the community spirit – well there might have been a bit of community spirit and there was laughter and we were tough, but it was still bloody awful. Harsh conditions make people harsh. That's what I remember.

My mum seemed really cross on that first day as she took me to work. She hardly said a word on the journey. But she told me later she felt scared of the big change coming and me not being around any more. She didn't want to leave me with strangers. She was trying to be tough so the two of us didn't blub all the way there; I think she was nervous, too, because she was out of her depth away from Hoxton.

I remember we walked up the long gentle slope as the road rises to the Angel and then headed down Pentonville Road towards Kings Cross station. This seemed a marvel to me, who'd never been on a train. All the houses down Pentonville Road were multi-occupied then, but they weren't as poor as we were. There were probably a few posh people who still had a whole house here and there. I can remember nannies setting off with babies in the biggest prams you've ever seen.

They stopped making the real giant prams between the wars, I think. These prams had huge curving springs so the baby would float on a cushion of air – well, that was the idea. There was a massive canvas hood too and the whole contraption looked about four feet high and five feet long. I remember thinking it was mad to have all that space for one little kid. And why the hell did prams always have to be black?

Come to think of it almost everything was black back then. I think it was a hangover from the fat little cook – that's what we used to call the old queen, Victoria. Just because she loved black, because her old man had died, we all had to have nothing but black for half a century.

Anyway, those big old prams were black and when they got dumped in the end or were sent to the second-hand man, they'd eventually end up in poorer areas. Then they'd get sold again a couple of times to poorer and poorer people and in the end they'd be cut up for their big back wheels to make kids' carts or even small carts used by adults to carry things around.

For the poorest, who had no cars and no vans nor access to them, it was murder to move your pots and pans if you needed to move house. Everyone relied on knowing someone with a cart who could help for a bob or two. Otherwise you'd have to lug it all yourself. We often saw a load of kids moving their mum's and dad's bed down Bethnal Green Road and no one took a blind bit of notice.

Chapter Nine

Anyone born after the Second World War would have been amazed at the number of hats I saw on that morning journey of mine all the way from the Kingsland Road to Marylebone Road. I don't think I saw a single person not wearing a hat – apart from a few kids and not many of them either, I can tell you. The odd little street Arab – that's what people called beggar children – was hatless, but for everyone else, going hatless would have been like going out without your knickers on!

Men wore straw hats in summer, if they were better off, and caps, trilbies, bowler hats, homburgs and all sorts the rest of the time. It was almost more of an obsession for men than women. The real toffs wore top hats of course. A lot of poor people paid more bleedin' attention to their hats than anything else. Your shoes might have had holes in them, but it wasn't decent to be out without a hat. I knew quite a few people who lived near us and I'd never seen them without a hat on. I remember bumping into one neighbour after saying hello every day for years, then discovering he was bald. I couldn't believe it. I hardly recognised him! The other thing about wearing a hat was that you didn't have to worry what your hair looked like. Some men got their hair cut properly but far more had their wives just hack it off short. Sometimes a hat covered up a right old mess. And I don't think many men washed their hair much. If you'd suggested they get some shampoo they'd probably punch you, because they were very sensitive about any suggestion that they were effeminate in any way.

You just didn't dare go out without a hat and better-off women had real fancy hats – covered in feathers they were and with lace all over the place. A lot of women wore veils and not because they were modest. It was supposed to be alluring. You see girls now with beautifully cut natural hair or dyed all sorts of funny colours and they spend a fortune on it. Well when I was a girl real hair was for your husband. Hats were for everyone else to see when you were out in public.

Anyway, there we were walking along Marylebone Road like a right pair of timorous Annies. I'd assumed my mum knew where we were going, but she suddenly darted across the pavement and asked someone for directions to Cavendish Square – the house I was to work in was just off the square.

We finally found it after a lot of doubling back and crossing and re-crossing various streets that all looked the same. It was a tall terraced house, very gloomy looking and seemed enormous to me. Just before we went to the door my mum said she'd got a surprise for me. It was a lovely bar of chocolate, which I knew she couldn't really afford. She said it was because I'd need the energy later on so I wasn't to eat it till the end of my first day.

My mum knew enough to know that we were not under any circumstances to go anywhere near the front door. She said we'd better find the door the tradesmen used. It's funny but my mum never questioned the fact that we were the ones who always had to bow and scrape. People didn't question things then. They all accepted that people should know their place. This was bloody silly in lots of ways, because it meant that poor people didn't push their kids to do better than they did. I think it was partly the church's fault, because they never helped the poor except to make them sing hymns and worry about the next life. What about this bloody life?

There didn't seem to be a way round the back of the house so we hung about for a bit wondering what to do until I spotted a little enamel sign on the railing with a black finger pointing to the basement. The sign said 'Deliveries'. So we thought we'd better go down into the area – the basement – and see what we would find there.

I remember a set of dingy stone steps that went into what looked like a deep dark hole. It was probably at least 15 feet down. At the bottom was a large window with miserable dark green paint on the woodwork. Next to it was a massive black door with a brass knocker and a brass plate that said 'Tradesmen Knock Twice'.

This made me laugh. What if you knocked twice and no one came? Were you supposed to never knock again that day and go away and come back the next day?

There was also a long chain which presumably went to a bell. We didn't even think of using that. If it said knock then we were going to knock. We knew our place which was to do whatever our betters told us to do!

We knocked and I wondered if we should knock twice but then thought we're not tradesmen so we'd better knock once or three times. The truth is we were both terrified. And even though it was spring – it was around the end of March or early April, I think – it was still cold.

We waited for ages and not a sound of anyone stirring. We looked at each other and I was about to say maybe we should go away when the door opened about two inches. I could see a little face or rather half a little face. It saw us and opened the door. Then it disappeared along a stone corridor and up some steps. We were left standing in a very cold corridor with a stone floor and two gaslights high up on the walls.

Anyone who remembers gaslight will remember how yellow it was – and dim compared to electricity. Well these were even dimmer than the average gaslight because the mantles needed changing. The mantle was a bit of silk that turned to dust when you first lit the lamp but didn't quite fall apart each subsequent time you lit it if you were careful. If you so much as breathed on it once it had been burned it crumbled, but it would last quite a long time so long as you just lit it each time and were careful not to brush it with the match.

The lamps in that basement definitely needed new mantles. They hardly cast any light at all and there were no windows. I remember looking down and thinking how big the stone slabs on the floor were. They were all crooked with big gaps between them and in one place there was even a small puddle. I thought: 'Blimey there's a river down here!'

But houses didn't have damp courses then, so if they were damp you had to put up with it. One of the little houses back in Hoxton was famous for having a stream under it. I'm not kidding. The bloke who owned it used to let the local kids have a look under his floorboards. It was just a trickle but it showed how the builders would get round a problem. They had made the floor a couple of feet higher than the floors in the houses either side so the water was further away – presumably just in case it rained a lot and the trickle suddenly turned into a small river!

There we were all on our own in that slimy corridor when a voice shouted 'Oi, yer can come up.' We went up the stairs, which were very bleak looking, narrow and made of stone. Then there was a small door into the hallway.

When we went through the door my eyes nearly fell out because that hallway was the grandest thing I'd ever seen. Looking back, of course it wasn't really grand at all. But it was miles bigger than the two rooms we had for the whole family.

The house seemed dark and scary to me with stairs all over the place. It still had old wooden panelling on some walls and half way up the stairs was a faded wall painting. I never took much notice of it at the time but these days people would have made a big fuss.

I had to live in. Seeing as I started as a maid of all work I got the worst room – tiny and right at the top of the house,

46

freezing in winter and boiling in summer. No rugs or carpets. Just a little metal bed, a curtain on the window and a stand with a jug of water for washing. In winter it would have a thin layer of ice on top.

But it was the first time I'd had my own room so I was excited. Little did I realise that the only thing I'd ever do in that room was sleep and I wouldn't even get much of that.

The servants had a separate narrow and very steep set of stairs right at the back of the house so the family wouldn't have to be bumping into us all the time.

The hall looked so luxurious with big pot plants, a tiled floor with a sort of intricate brown pattern over it and dark heavy embossed paper on the walls. It was painted one colour below the dado rail and another above, but both colours were pretty dingy. People seemed to love dingy in those days – another Victorian hangover!

There were several giant pot plants along that hall as well as a table with a mirror above it. The table had what we called a Turkey rug draped across it. I swear that hall must have been unchanged since the 1880s or even earlier. There were several big pieces of mahogany furniture including a massive cupboard with another mirror. It must have weighed a ton. Later, I discovered it was just to put hats and gloves in.

I also later learned that for the maid it was a serious offence to put visitors' coats on the pegs in the cupboard and their gloves tucked in just underneath them. That wasn't allowed. The gloves had to go in the narrow drawer underneath the main cupboard.

This was typical of pretty much everything you learned when you went into service. There were picky time-wasting rules about almost everything and things were done in a certain way just because they'd always been done like that even if there was a quicker and easier way to do them.

At one end of this huge hall there was a massive front door

with beautiful red, yellow and green coloured glass in a window above it. At the other end of the hall there was what looked like a bloomin' glass house.

I found out later on that that was what it really was. A lot of houses then had a first floor room above the garden that was made mostly of glass and held up on steel pillars. The Victorians and Edwardians loved indoor plants and the bigger and more exotic the better. Looking after the buggers was to be one of my tasks.

This was a smaller house, although on that first day it seemed huge to me. In much bigger houses than this one I might never have met the lady of the house or the gentleman (that was the way we had to refer to them) because I would have been under the cook, if my duties were in the kitchen; or under the house-keeper if I'd been going as a housemaid. In bigger houses the servants always interviewed the new servants, as I later discovered. But here I was going to be the maid of all work so the great lady was going to demean herself and interview us personally.

The woman who was about to meet us was Mrs Williams. Like all middle-class women in earlier times she didn't do anything beyond drink tea and go shopping, go to the toilet, go to bed, get up and then off we go again. Her husband was away a lot of the time, we were told. I only found out what he did when he came back from lord knows where, and only a few weeks before I left.

So there we were in the hall when like a bloody great ship Mrs Williams comes sailing out of a door near where we were standing – a door I hadn't even noticed. She said good morning to us and we said good morning back and my poor old mum was so overcome that she even did a little curtsey. It broke my heart to see it, but it's hard for anyone who wasn't alive then to realise how overawed poor people like us were by the well off. Mrs Williams seemed like the Queen of bloody England to us because we'd never got into close quarters before with anyone who lived like this.

Mrs Williams would probably have seemed very common I'm sure to someone with a title and a really big house – then she'd have been curtseying like mad to anyone above her just as we were. But that's how it all seemed to work. The higher up you were the more people you could enjoy looking down on. We were timid and afraid of people with money and big houses.

This time we had some excuse because Mum wanted Mrs W to give me a job. We'd have stood on our heads or danced a jig for her that day.

After a minute when she sort of looked us up and down, she asked us to follow her and we went into an even more impressive room than the hallway. The ceiling there seemed about 20 feet up and everywhere there were cabinets with ornaments, tables covered with little boxes, plants and all sorts of stuff, most of which I'd never seen the likes of before.

I had a quick look round when Mrs Williams wasn't looking. My mum had said that the quality, as she used to call them, hated poor people looking at their things because it made them think you were going to try to nick everything!

Mrs W must have been wearing about eight miles of lace and bombazine and jewellery. She seemed huge to me. Though a lot of women's clothes had slimmed down by this time and skirts were a bit shorter – a few inches above your ankles – she was dressed in a very old-fashioned style. Her skirts and underskirts and petticoats and lord knows what all reached to the ground. She sat down behind a small desk with lots of little drawers in it and then swivelled round to look at us. There were no seats for us and I quickly discovered that sitting in the presence of your employer was just about the worst thing you could do apart from murdering someone. So we stood there in that gloomy room with its huge curtains half covering the huge bay windows – they kept the light out to stop the furniture fading – while she asked me questions.

She asked if I had experience in a kitchen and if I cleaned and mended at home. I said yes ma'am to everything although I was so nervous I didn't really take in much of what she said. The only question that really stuck was: 'Can you read and write?' I was really proud when I told her I could and actually I was really good at reading, writing and arithmetic. If I'd been born 60 years later I'm sure I'd have gone somewhere in life. I was born too soon!

She then told me that I was very lucky because in many houses they would have deducted the cost of my uniform and my extra aprons from my first wages, but that she wasn't going to do that because I could have the uniform that the last girl had. She was sure we were about the same size. She also said that I was lucky as I'd get board and lodging. I should realise and be grateful because many girls wouldn't get such an opportunity. I was still babbling, 'Yes ma'am, thank you ma'am,' at every opportunity – once I even said it before she'd finished the latest in her list of all the wonderful things I was soon to enjoy.

She never spoke a word to my mum – didn't even look at her. At the end of ten minutes she just said: 'Start on Monday.' She never mentioned if there were other servants or what the hours would be or how I might get trained. She probably just thought I would pick it up as I went along. She didn't ask if *we* wanted to know anything – not that we would have dared to ask.

Then out of nowhere The Boots – the boy who'd opened the tradesmen's door to us – stuck his head round the hall door and made a little wave. We sort of bobbed a bit to Mrs W, who was concentrating on something on her desk, then turned round quickly and shuffled out.

I got a ticking off for that on the following Monday because we'd turned our backs on Mrs W to get out of the room which we shouldn't have. Cook told me a few days after I'd started that Mrs W had decided to overlook this as I was new and didn't know any better.

I was to be a maid of all work, but there was a cook cum housekeeper – that was Mrs James – and The Boots as I called the boy we'd seen. But I was supposed to help Mrs James with some of the kitchen tasks and I did when I wasn't being chivvied by her majesty.

I wasn't shown where I'd be sleeping when we had that interview because the idea that I might have turned the job down for any reason wouldn't have occurred for a minute to Mrs W. This was 1925 and servants were still ten a penny. No thought of showing a prospective servant their bedroom and saying 'Is this all right for you?' The only thing we were told apart from when I was to start was how much I'd be paid. It was ten shillings a week which seemed a fortune to me and actually wasn't bad for a completely inexperienced skivvy.

In the months to come I have to admit that I didn't get treated like dirt by Mrs W and she probably wasn't a bad old sort really, but servants were servants and there was an idea at the time that if you were too nice to servants they would take advantage. So in the time I was with her, Mrs W never smiled at me or asked how I was, but then she didn't lock me in the coal hole either or throw things at me or scream at me or slap me – all those things happened to other maids I knew.

Chapter Ten

After that first interview as Mum and I walked slowly back to the Angel and Pentonville she talked about what a great chance this was for me. Mum thought Mrs W probably wasn't too bad either and said that for her the house was like a dream. For me to be able just to live there even as servant was really something. She said she thought that one reason I'd got the job was that I was good at reading and writing. It was one of the few questions Mrs W had asked.

But we both felt a bit silly as I'd gone with a bag of my things ready to stay and start work but we'd been sent away till Monday. We shared my bar of chocolate on the way back.

I told Mum I was really nervous and worried I wouldn't be able to do all the different jobs I'd have to do. But Mum pointed out I hadn't just been learning to read and write at school – I'd been taught to iron and sew. All the board schools in those days spent half their time showing girls how to do chores.

If someone had said, 'But women should be able to have careers in banking and politics, teaching and medicine, and men should help with the household chores,' they'd have been laughed at. But the point is no one would have said anything against the system. It would have been unthinkable – like doing your washing on a Tuesday instead of a Monday.

You wouldn't believe how conservative people were. Girls were going to be mums. If they did work, they had jobs that were considered suitable. I could have gone to work in a factory until I married but that was about the most revolutionary thing you could choose. The East End had two or three match factories where they employed a lot of women, but despite the fact that it paid better than being a servant, a lot of people – including my family – thought it was all wrong, a girl working in a factory. There you are you see – conservatism.

Working in service is what you did and on that walk back home through Islington my mum said to me that if I behaved and worked hard I might rise to become a head housemaid or even a parlour maid. Makes people laugh when I tell them now – the idea that you might think being a head housemaid was something great, but back then for a poor girl it was something to be aimed at.

That makes me sad when I look back. Why didn't we try to be lawyers and doctors and such like? Why? Because we had no money and no connections and it just wasn't done.

When I look back and compare what girls had then with what they have now I'm amazed – and delighted. By the 1970s even poor girls could go to university, have lots of boyfriends and not even think of getting married. They became doctors and bankers and good luck to them. I think it's great but I can't forget all those girls who were wasted on early marriages, endless children and poverty – and skivvying for the rich. Even when I was middle aged in the 1960s there was a bit of the old nonsense left. I remember an old man telling me that his wife was really intelligent but hadn't had an education. If she'd had an education, he said, she could even have been a secretary – as if being a secretary was something incredible!

So there I was back in Hoxton with Mum and my brothers and sisters and they were all excited about my new job. I'm not sure I was excited, but I kept saying to myself that skivvying at home and sharing a bed with the others had to be worse than being in a big smart house with my own little room and plenty of good food. I sort of convinced myself that I'd have money, friends, time off and roast beef every day. I thought I'd be starting at 9.00 am every day because I'd been told to be at the house on Monday at 9.00 am. I was a right mug!

Chapter Eleven

Monday came around. I got up really early and didn't wake the others – it would have taken a bomb to wake them anyway. We were all so used to sleeping in the same room that no one noticed anyone moving around or getting up extra early. Like so many difficult things you accepted having no space because you'd never known anything else.

I had put out my dress and pinafore. The dress had a few patches but the pinafore was good. I gathered up a spare dress my mum had got me specially at the old clothes market, along with my underthings – I'm not going to tell you what they were like or the state they were in! And I had a coat, two shirts and a spare pair of shoes.

I didn't have a toothbrush. No one I knew had one. We didn't get sweets much and everyone thought that you either had good teeth or you didn't; that it was the luck of birth and nothing to do with looking after them.

Teeth were such a nuisance and cause of trouble and pain that a lot of girls as a marriage present got a set of false gnashers. The idea was that your new husband didn't have to worry that when you got toothache he'd have to pay for a dentist. Poor people feared dentists. In fact some of the old boys thought a dentist was a sort of con artist like a card sharp.

And hospitals were only for when you were dying. You'd only go if you were at death's door. Babies came into the world without even a nod from the doctors. We all knew who could come and help when a woman went into labour. People would have thought you were mad to go off and get a stranger even if he said he was a doctor. This was before antibiotics, remember, so doctors were pretty useless anyway.

If you were taken bad you either got better or died and no one thought any doctor could do much about it. I remember one man with about ten children had been coughing a lot. Someone told him there was a free day at St Thomas's hospital over Lambeth way. Well, off he trotted and was told he had consumption and that he should try living abroad for a couple of years! That made me laugh. Doctors were supposed to be intelligent but I've thought they were idiots ever since I heard that – fancy telling a man with ten kids and no job to go and live in the south of France.

Another time, a doctor came to someone in the square – Hoxton Square I mean. He saved a kid by cutting him open on the kitchen table after knocking him out with a cloth covered in ether. The doctor did it for nothing but nearly got lynched as everyone thought he'd murdered the boy. But then the boy survived and used to go round showing all the other kids what looked like a pink worm in a jar. It was his appendix. But that didn't convince the locals.

So there I was getting dressed and shivering when Mum came in with a candle. It was almost light outside but very dingy and overcast and the little windows we had didn't let much light in at the best of times. The mist from the river combined with all the soot and smog made most days a bit gloomy, except sometimes when the wind blew on a bright day in summer and all the fog disappeared down the estuary.

I can still see Mum with her candle moving about quietly and casting big shadows. We went in the other room and sat by the little range. This had a tiny fire at one end held in by horizontal iron bars and the ash fell through the bars on to the brick hearth below. The other end was a small cast iron oven with a hotplate on top. That's where we did our cooking, such as it was, and as I say, it was also where Mum and Dad slept.

Mum and I had a bit of whispered chat and I had bread and butter with white sugar, which was another lovely treat. Then at about quarter-past seven I set off – but this time on my own.

That gave me an hour and three-quarters to walk there. I didn't have the bus fare and mum thought I'd be shy about hopping on a cart tailboard. She was right. I put on my coat, picked up my little bag and off I went.

I wasn't one of those kids who thought their mum and dad were keen to get rid of them because of the expense of keeping them. Kids like that often couldn't wait to get away because, although they would be drudging every day, at least they were going to get paid for it and would have a bit of space to themselves. True, I was looking forward to a bit of space myself – I'd have my own room after all – but I knew I would miss my family, for all their noise. My biggest worry was that I wouldn't be able to do the job and that I'd be lonely. I was so inexperienced except in the ways of the East End – and the way we did things in the East End was not the way they did them in the West End.

The Kingsland Road and Pentonville Road were as busy as ever as I toddled along. Even more this time it seemed to me that the traffic just went where it wanted to. I don't remember any traffic lights. There might have been a few in London by then, but if there were, I don't think people took much notice of them. The carts and cars and lorries just got out of each other's way as best they could and junctions could be a right tangle, but we muddled by as Londoners always had.

Although it was 1925 you still saw quite a few men who had been badly injured in the Great War. They got along like everyone else. I saw one that morning. He was blind. He stood near the Angel junction with New North Road selling matches. I know a lot of soldiers felt that they were forgotten after the war. They were a bit of an embarrassment, really. I suppose soldiers always are when hostilities have ended and the warring governments try to get on with each other again. Legless and eyeless soldiers are a nasty reminder.

I was nervous going along and kept putting my hand up to my hat, which I thought was very smart and was terrified of losing. Really it was a shabby little black thing with a few feathers, but I loved it and it made me feel really grown up.

If I'm giving the impression that I was a sad, shy, retiring little creature I should say that I could be really cheeky too. If anyone said anything to me I would always answer them back. And like a lot of working-class people back then I had a selection of some very nice ripe words when it came to effing and blinding. It wasn't the Billingsgate fishwives you had to worry about, it was the girl from Hoxton. But I'd been warned about this. Whatever you do Rose, don't lose your bleedin' temper or you'll get the sack. As I went along I thought: I'm going to make a go of this . . .

I was making good time along the Marylebone Road. When I cut down towards Oxford Street I noticed the usual smart houses, the cleaner streets and something I hadn't really noticed before: just how much better dressed people were.

Clothes were much more of a uniform then. Gentlemen often wore tails and a top hat with high collars and very shiny shoes with the thinnest soles. Working men might have a soft hat or a cap and rough jackets and moleskin trousers and they almost always wore a choker, a sort of white scarf knotted round the neck.

Where I was going now toffs were far more common than in other parts of London. They carried canes and had a sort of arrogant walk you don't see today. They really did walk with their heads slightly tilted back so they could look down their noses at you. They would have known straight away that I was a poor girl from my shabby second-hand clothes. But I just accepted that this was the way of the world, so I didn't feel sorry for myself.

A few months later, after I'd settled into the job a bit, a toff spoke to me as I walked along the road one afternoon and I was so amazed at the way he pronounced his words that I stared at him open-mouthed. After a pause, he just sort of wandered off. I can still recall exactly how he pronounced his words – it was as if he said 'kesh' instead of cash, meaning money.

The worst part of knowing nothing is you don't even know how ignorant you are. My first day in that house showed me that I didn't know a bloody thing, and this first house was nothing compared to the bigger houses I worked in later on.

So there I was going down those stone steps again on my first Monday. The Boots let me in and said, 'Cook's in there,' pointing at another door I hadn't noticed before.

I knocked and waited. Nothing. I knocked again and after a while heard a bit of shuffling and the door opened.

I thought she'd be a great big woman because she was dealing with food all day, but she was a quite a skinny thing. She was aged about 50 I should think, though she seemed about 90 to me. She looked me up and down and said, 'I'll show you where you'll sleep.'

I was so overwhelmed by all these new experiences that I just nodded nervously. She probably took me for an idiot.

It was up about ten flights. As we climbed the back stairs together she never said another word until we got to a narrow green door that you had to duck to get through. Inside I found myself in a room about eight feet square with an iron bed, a tiny fireplace that had room for two or three lumps of coal, a small painted cupboard, a chair and a small window that was too high up for me to see out of without standing on the chair. Without a word Cook left me and I listened to her clattering down the stairs.

I looked around and felt a bit of confidence coming back. I thought I was getting somewhere in life as I'd never had a room of my own before. The novelty quickly wore off, I can tell you.

At home we'd usually put more clothes on to go to bed than when we were up and around. We also had each other to keep warm. Even though the worst of the winter was past, my biggest memory of this little room was to be how cold I got at night. I didn't know yet but that little fire I looked at so hopefully was never lit. It had never been lit in anyone's memory.

There was nothing on the walls but then most people didn't have much on their walls – maybe a print from the Boer War or a picture of Victoria if you were patriotic. We had nothing on our walls at home, so I wasn't expecting a flippin' art gallery.

What had just happened to me was typical of what often happened when you started a new job in domestic service. You got hardly a word at the start and no help with what you were supposed to do next. I used to think it was deliberate, so the people who were in charge of you could shout at you for not knowing what to do. But perhaps the truth is everyone back then assumed you would just know without being told. And if you didn't know, people put you down as an idiot. So the trick was to learn fast – very fast.

I put my small bag down on the bare floorboards in that room and had a look round. I say bare floorboards but they were actually painted black. I put my spare underclothes, my coat and stockings in the cupboard, hopped on the chair and looked out the grubby window. Could hardly see a bloomin' thing. Apart from the fact that the glass was filthy, all it over-looked was rooftops and slates anyway. I jumped down and sat on the edge of the bed, thinking 'What do I do now?' I thought maybe I don't have to do anything until later.

And then I noticed the silence. I wasn't used to silence, what with my brothers and sisters constantly talking and shouting and rushing in and out; but here it was very quiet. I was just thinking about this when the door opened and The Boots stuck his head in and said: 'She wants you in the kitchen.' He then just turned and disappeared.

There was something about the way he said it that made me think, 'You're in trouble my girl.' I clattered down the stairs and sure enough Cook was in a bad mood. I can't remember exactly what she said but it had lots of 'lazy good-for-nothing workhouse skivvies' in it. Then she had a go at me for not being in my uniform. I wasn't a really timid girl as I've said but I was feeling a bit tearful by now. Then suddenly she softened a bit and said to The Boots, 'Did you give her Nellie's uniform?'

The Boots ran off straight away and came back with a dirty muslin bag with a morning blue dress and an afternoon black dress and half a dozen aprons in it. There was a big apron for the morning that was to be worn with the blue dress and a smaller apron for the afternoon when I was supposed to change into the black dress.

'Off you go then and get changed,' said Cook as if she'd never said a harsh word in her life. So off I went. I didn't hang about this time. I shot down those back stairs again once I was dressed as if my life depended on it.

Cook then told me what I had to do that day. It was such a long list that I couldn't remember half what she said, but I did get the first bit.

She gave me a big slightly crumbly block of white stuff. This was hearthstone cleaner which was made from a special kind of stone. She told me to clean and whiten the steps at the front of the house with it and then to do the whole of the back stairs right to the top. She gave me a bucket of water and said I should do a few steps at a time with the cloth and the water and then rub them with the hearthstone, the white block, until each step was gleaming.

I went up the area steps with my cloth, my bucket and block and got to work and I think I made a good job of it, but it didn't half hurt my bloody knees. I never understood why someone didn't invent a brush on a long stick for steps and a block on a similarly long stick, but they didn't.

I think employers of domestic servants only thought they were getting their money's worth if the servants were continually on their knees. You'd be amazed how many jobs had to be done in this painful way. This is why so many housemaids suffered from 'housemaid's knee'. After a couple of months

Cook told me to sew a couple of cotton pads to the knees of my stockings or, as she put it, 'You'll be useless to us in no time at all.'

Your knees could get so bad from resting on them all the time that you really couldn't work any more. Housemaid's knee was some form of arthritis and it was crippling if you got it bad.

There were about six or eight steps at the front. When I'd finished Cook came and had a quick look. She told me they'd do, but that next time I should look for every mark and stain and get rid of them with the hearthstone. They wanted the steps to look absolutely white – every day. When she went off I had another look at what I'd done and they looked pretty good to me. But I made a mental note to be done with it and whiten every bit of the steps and not just the marks.

My next major job was to do the same thing for the servants' steps at the back of the house. Though they were narrow there were a hell of a lot of them. They went from the basement up six floors, so I wasn't looking forward to that. I was about to get down on my knees and start on them when Cook told me she needed a hand getting ready for lunch and that the steps would have to wait. I was relieved but only for a minute because helping Cook with lunch was a nightmare as I had no experience of a big kitchen. At home we had only a few pots and pans and plates – not the mountain of stuff they had in this kitchen.

And then there was Cook. She was probably a nice woman at heart but my memory of her is that she was almost always in a bad mood. She only had me to work for her – well, me and The Boots. In a really big house, as I later found out, the cook might be in charge of three or four servants and the mistress of the house would almost defer to her about menus and that kind of thing. Despite the fact that servants were seen as lower class, common and stupid by their employers, generally there was a slightly different attitude to the cook. In a big house – and in most small ones – there was a tradition that the mistress of the house never entered the kitchen without knocking first.

Can you believe that? I still don't quite know why this was. I can't believe it was out of respect. It might have been so that the cook had time to get rid of the scullery maid and kitchen maid before the mistress came in, because those really lowly servants were supposed to be completely invisible.

In the kitchen on that first morning I started by chopping every kind of vegetable. Cook amazed me by how quick she was. I was also shown how to lay out the big deal table ready for Cook to get to work. You had to put out masses of different cutting knives, wooden spoons, metal spoons, spatulas, sieves, colanders, saucepans, sauceboats, salt, pepper and other condiments and you had to do it neatly and in the right order or woe betide. Of course I made a mess of it that first day because I hadn't a clue what I was doing. Cook only grumbled under her breath at me. I tried really hard to remember, because I knew I'd have to do it again next day and every day.

It wasn't a massive kitchen but it was big compared to anything I'd ever seen. Cook dodged back and forth organising everything in a way that dazzled me. I wasn't much help to her and she kept saying I was too slow. But I warmed to her a bit when she started to sing at the top of her voice what I later discovered were rebel Irish songs.

Later on when I got to know her a bit better she used to make me laugh. At 8.30 each morning she'd say, 'The old Kipper will be down in a minute – get out of it now.' That meant I was to make myself scarce. Cook had a lot of odd phrases like that. I'd then go into the pantry which was always freezing, even in summer, to keep the food fresh. The floor was thick slate and the shelves were all slate lined and there was wire over the window and no glass at all. I'd sit there on an old wooden chair and a few minutes later I'd hear the mistress come clip-clopping down into the kitchen. She'd look at what Cook had planned for the day and either agree with it or change a few things. That was the tradition in all but the smallest houses. I used to hear them talking through the great heavy door and think, 'Why the bloody hell am I not fit to be seen?' It was like being a leper. But every morning I had to sit there until the great lady had buggered off back upstairs.

Cook called the mistress 'Kipper' because she always looked so brown with a ton of makeup on. She also wore a lot of brown – a popular colour back then. I suppose after decades spent copying old Queen Victoria, who only wore black, they thought dark brown was a bit modern and racy – but not so modern as to be not respectable. That was a big thing in those days – you had to be respectable.

When I looked back much later on and long after I'd left that house, I felt a bit sorry for the old Kipper because she was trying to do the whole servant business as if she was an aristocrat and she didn't really have the means to do it. Like a lot of people – I'd say almost everyone then – she was obsessed with the idea that people would not think she was as grand as she thought she was herself. So although she only had Cook, me and The Boots, she acted as if she had 30 servants and owned half of Yorkshire.

I was tired by mid morning that first day as it seemed endless, but I kept quiet and though I made lots of mistakes I was determined not to make so many the next day. And I think Cook realised I wasn't completely stupid and so was quite nice to me, really. I think she sensed I wanted to get it right and she was the same. Like me she was a bit of a rebel inside but took pride in her work. She showed me how to put out all the implements each day in their allotted places; kitchens in the early twentieth century had far more knives and different kinds of pan than they do now. The pans were cast iron or copper and really heavy. You'd never believe the number they used then – big copper pots you could put a sheep in down to the tiniest pots for a single egg. And they all had to be cleaned every day, all 26 of them.

I quickly learned to put out the ones I thought Cook would need as well as all the necessary ingredients.

As soon as she was ready and happy with what I'd put out she'd say, 'Off you go,' and I'd start chopping and slicing like a mad thing. Then when that was done I was sent off to the back stairs to carry on cleaning the steps. What a slow painful climb that was – more than 100 steps on my aching knees. I also oiled the narrow wooden banister with linseed.

The steps and banisters took about three hours and I was exhausted at the end of it.

When I'd finished I had a bit of dinner down in the kitchen with Cook. We always called lunch 'dinner' in those days. All ordinary people did. I had it with The Boots and Cook, the three of us not saying a word. The Boots ate as fast as I'd ever seen anyone eat – and I'd seen some bloody fast eating, I can tell you. He was called Tommy and he was scruffiest little blighter I'd ever come across. I think Mrs W hardly paid him anything and he lived in a space under the stairs. It really was under the stairs, but the stairs were big so it actually wasn't such a bad little room in a way. Mrs James didn't live in but I did so it was just The Boots and me. It was an unusual arrangement because a house that big would normally have had more servants and I wondered if they were actually a bit short of cash. I have no idea why but The Boots also had to eat sitting on a stool. I'm sure it wouldn't have been Cook who insisted on it. It would have been a rule of the house to create a sort of social hierarchy even among the lowly.

As I sat there munching I felt really awkward and found it hard to swallow because my swallows sounded so loud! Apart from my gulps all I could hear was the big clock on the wall. But the dinner was lovely. I'd never had such a delicious meal and I've never forgotten it. It made me think for a bit that there might be something to this servant business after all. I had a chop, some lovely mashed potato and a huge pile of cabbage. And then Cook asked me if I wanted more. I nearly fell over. There was never any question of more at home. She dolloped another load of cabbage on my plate and a ton of spuds. Not another chop, but I didn't mind a bit; I was in clover. 'You'd better eat up girl,' she said. 'You've got a lot more work to do today.'

She wasn't joking, either. As soon as I finished eating I had to clean the pans and the plates and knives and forks from our dinner and from Mrs W's breakfast. The pans – and as I've said there were loads of them – were sprinkled with what looked like brick dust. I believe it was special sort of sand, and then you tipped a bit of vinegar in. You rubbed it with your hands till the pans were scoured out nicely. There were no detergents.

I did it as if my life depended on it. I regretted this later when I noticed that I'd virtually skinned my fingers. I did the cutlery next in the big old lead-lined sink. A huge amount of the metal in those old kitchens was lead, especially the pipes. No one worried because we didn't know it was bad for you. We must have eaten and drunk loads of small bits of it and damaged our brains!

I was told never to soak the knives and forks because it would make the handles fall off. They had to be cleaned using more of that bloody painful sand, but this time mixed with oil. After they'd been cleaned with this mix they were polished with a dry cloth. Plates were cleaned with soap that came in great big tins. Or sometimes we'd collect old remnants of soap in a wire basket which was then dipped in the water and sloshed about until there was enough soap to do the knives. Very little was wasted. You rinsed the plates in clean water in another sink and then put them in a rack to dry.

Though not as bad as the vinegar and oil and sand, the soap was enough to turn your hands raw. Then there was the cleaning soda which was sometimes used – it was like bloody acid. The truth is that everything we used made our hands a mess because there were no protective gloves then. You just had to try to put up with it.

Many girls couldn't – their hands got so bad they had to leave and go home. There they weren't always welcome because, if they didn't work, they cost their families money to keep. Many girls didn't have a home like mine where, though we were skint, my mum wouldn't have dreamed of letting on that we were a burden. I met lots of girls terrified they'd be sacked and have to go home because their mums didn't want them back or because they hated it at home.

As a friend I made a bit later on once said to me: 'I loved it when I started work – I might have had to skivvy for a load of toffs but at least they fed me and I had my own bed and a bit of decent food. At home I was an unpaid servant and the food was terrible and my mum and dad were always at me to get out of the house.'

Anyway, the rest of that first day was the busiest in my life. After doing the dishes and pans I had to put the pans upside-down on a shelf: they had to be half hanging off the edge of the shelf to let them air. You were in big trouble if you forgot to do that.

Then, without a pause, I was back on the back stairs with that big block of bloody whitener gradually making my way up on my knees. I got absorbed in the work after a bit – it was the only way to get through it. Then The Boots came to get me to wash up after her ladyship, Mrs W, had had lunch.

She'd had some friends in. The servants always, in my experience, had their lunch before the family had theirs. It was because we got up so early and the family would get up much later. We had our dinner at 11.30 am or 12.00 and they had theirs at 1.00 or 1.30 pm or whenever they told us they wanted it.

As there were only three of us below stairs my duties varied a bit more day to day than they would later on in bigger houses. I think on that first day they got me to do the simpler things – cleaning the front steps and back steps, getting the vegetables ready, washing up; but there were other jobs and I only gradually learned how to do them.

The front steps had to be cleaned and whitened every day but the back steps, the servants', were done only once a week. The brass furniture on the front door was done every day with more hand-ruining brick dust, only this time mixed with linseed oil.

All afternoon of that first day when I wasn't washing up I worked on those bloody back stairs and then I ran down to help prepare the evening meal.

I got told off for not changing my uniform. That was another rule wherever you worked – one uniform for the morning and another for the afternoon. So I ran back up the stairs in a right tizz and fluster. I got the other uniform that The Boots had given me and got into it as fast as I could. It had obviously been in a bag since my predecessor had worn it because it was very damp. Also it didn't fit very well. That wouldn't matter much as so many people wore second-hand clothes or hand-me-downs in the 1920s. It was a real surprise when you saw someone with clothes that did fit.

We were all so skinny back then but I was even skinnier than most. I was 15 and I think I was only starting puberty. Modern girls start at about 12 years, I think, but we were later because we were half starved and mostly underweight.

So back down I went in my damp afternoon uniform. Cook told me I'd be waiting at the table that evening which was scary as I hadn't a clue what to do.

'Just take each dish in as I give it to you,' said Cook, 'and she'll point to where she wants it.' But first I had to go up with the knives and forks and plates and lay the table. Cook showed me how and it wasn't that complicated.

This would never have happened in a bigger house – I'd have not been allowed within a mile of the dining room or any other room where the family spent any time. In bigger houses, there was a strict split between front-of-house servants – butlers and footmen and parlour maids and housemaids – and back-of-house where the kitchen and scullery maids worked. Smaller houses muddled all this up more because they had to. For a maid of all work like me the name meant what it said: I was going to be doing the whole lot – I mean the work of parlour maid, waiting at table, as well as kitchen maid and housemaid.

In very grand houses you laid the table and measured the distances between the plates, the flowers and the candles, and then the butler would check the distances and you'd be in big trouble if they were wrong. Mrs W tried to copy all this sort of thing but it was always a pale imitation.

So I laid the table for five and went back downstairs. Half an hour later the little bell on the kitchen wall marked 'Dining Room' shook like there was a gale blowing. The noise nearly threw me into a fit. I was shaking as I was sent up with a tray and several dishes on it.

But the old Kipper – her ladyship – did just what Cook said she would. She pointed to various places and I put the dishes down where she pointed. Then I went out backwards. You didn't have to bow and scrape as you went into reverse but they would have loved it if you had! The ideal was that you sort of floated out like a fairy.

That morning I'd been told at length about the etiquette of getting into a room and out of it when the family were there. You could never turn your back on them so you went out in reverse and there was a skill in not knocking things over on the way. On my first day of course I wasn't too good at walking backwards. So there I was going in reverse with the tray when there was a terrific thud and I realised I'd walked into the door which of course I'd closed after me when I'd gone in. The funny thing was that The Kipper never looked round or said a word. She carried on talking in a slightly lah-di-dah voice to the two men and two women who were sitting there with her. You see, there were just as many rules for employers as for servants and The Kipper wasn't going to lower herself by noticing that I'd had a mishap on the way out.

They didn't have wine in that house or any alcohol with their meals. I think she was a teetotaller and a bit religious too. You always knew the religious ones. They were really hard on the servants and kept a beady eye on them when they had time off. I later found out that The Kipper had told Cook that on my afternoon off I was to be told only to go to Kensington Gardens and not Hyde Park which, she insisted, was not suitable for a young girl. I didn't know it at the time but girls used to pay guardsmen sixpence or a shilling to escort them round the park for half an hour, which was a thing our employers thought very immoral. And Hyde Park had a reputation for prostitution.

Early that evening I helped get tea ready for Cook, The Boots and me. Tea didn't mean cakes; it meant more spuds and some liver – tea was what the servants' evening meal was always called. Dinner was the family's evening meal.

So I washed up after our tea and then again after the family dinner. I'd worked pretty hard as a child when I wasn't at school helping Mum and running errands and so on, but after tidying that kitchen at about nine that first evening I was so tired I didn't know my own name. At one point standing over the sink my knees buckled under me for a split second as I fell asleep. I also noticed a sort of red stain coming off my fingertips and it was only when I had a good look at them that I noticed blood sort of seeping through the skin. But I still had to finish. It was only then that I was sent to bed by Cook and told not to stay up a minute longer. 'You'll be no good to anyone tomorrow if you don't go to sleep straight away,' she said – which was hilarious because there's no way I could have stayed up for a minute longer, I was so tired. I had no magazines or books to read anyway and my room was freezing.

I had a couple of blankets on the bed so I took my apron and dress off and then put my spare clothes on with my outdoor coat on top of the blankets.

I didn't sleep well. I just couldn't warm up. All night at that time you would hear church bells striking the hours across London. Some seemed miles away and I never liked them. They sounded very sad when you were all alone in the dark. Like ghosts they were. Eventually in fact I got up in the night and put my coat on properly and then got back into bed. At last I was warm enough to sleep.

A few weeks later I was given a hot water bottle. I think I wasn't given it at first because The Kipper wanted to be sure I was planning to stay and wouldn't run off with her precious water bottle. As there were no bathrooms for the servants or running water at the top of the house I used to use the water from my hot water bottle in the morning to have a little wash.

Chapter Twelve

On my first morning The Boots woke me and said I'd catch it as I was late. I discovered it was half past five and I should have been up at five. All the time I worked in that first house I marvelled at how The Boots was always awake first and never seemed to be tired.

After wake-up calls for the first few days you were expected just to get up at the right time on your own and without an alarm and you'd be amazed how quickly you could do it when you knew you'd be in trouble if you didn't.

My routine was really about to get going. That first day, though bloomin' exhausting, had been easy compared to what I was going to have to do as the weeks went by.

The Kipper was still having fires despite it being spring, so I had to clean all the grates each morning. I was sent to the brush cupboard, which was built into the thickness of the basement wall. The cupboard looked about 500 years old to me. It was a windowless walk-in room, tall, thin and brick lined. There was a huge collection of brushes of all kinds: carpet brushes, wall brushes, even saucepan and curtain brushes. They came in every size imaginable. I was baffled.

I asked which brush I should use and Cook soon saw me right.

Cook never talked much, but she wasn't too snappy. Some cooks and many housekeepers could be dragons, as I found out in future jobs. Anyway, I had my little brush for the hearth and a bucket with a hinged lid for the ash and cinders. Cook told me to keep the bigger pieces of cinder in the grate to start the new fire with and only to take out the smaller pieces and the ash. The sitting room fire was first.

The trick with cleaning a grate is not to throw up any dust if you can avoid it so you use gentle movements. The fireplaces were definitely one of the worst jobs. You had to clean the bars of the grate with emery paper to get the black off and most of it didn't go on your emery paper, it went on you. Then you polished the bars with a bit of leather till they gleamed.

Having cleaned the grate I then carried up a load of wood and a bucket of coal from the basement to lay the fire ready to be lit; then I went back to the brush cupboard for a duster and a carpet brush. The carpet brush seemed hardly different to the hearth brush but in those days there were tiny differences between all sorts of household tools. Nothing was standardised.

Then I started to clean the carpet on my knees. They had one big carpet in the middle of the room rather than a fitted carpet. No one had fitted carpets then. You try cleaning a 15-foot-square rug on your knees with red raw hands. They'd bled on my sheets the night before and were still very sore. Again, I never worked out why they couldn't have long-handled brushes for this work.

After the sitting room I had to do the drawing room grate and carpet in the same way, and then the dining room as well. Carpet sweepers and Hoovers were available by this time but people hated change and servants were cheaper and gave you more status. I once heard an old lady say: 'Vacuum cleaners, my dear. They are so dreadfully suburban'!

Then I found myself in the hall. There I had to clean the big rubbery leaves of all those bloody plants.

By 7.30 am I'd finished all the living rooms, their carpets and fires and the plants. I was then allowed a cup of tea and a quick sit down in the kitchen. After that I was outside the house again on my knees whitening those front steps and polishing the brass again. Next job was to take The Kipper's tea up to her. Knock on the door, wait for a grunt (because that was all I ever got), walk in and place the tea on the bedside table, curtsey and then reverse out. Like Cinderella.

After the first few days she started saying, 'Rose, don't be gloomy,' as I reversed out of the room having delivered the tea. From then on she said the same thing once or twice a week till the day I left.

First time I saw The Kipper in bed I nearly fainted. She had a ton of white sticky stuff on her face and her hair seemed to be in a velvet bag. She was so white she looked like she'd been dead for a week. So mornings she was not at her best. This made me feel much better about being sent to the pantry when she came down to discuss the day's doings with Cook. I thought, 'You might not want to see me, love, but I definitely don't want to see you!'

But after taking the tea in I'd go back downstairs and the daily round would carry on.

The Boots used to have tea with us, sitting on his stool, but for breakfast he used to sit on his own in a little cupboard room off the kitchen. There he was supposed to clean the shoes: Cook's shoes and The Kipper's and anyone else's who was staying, which did happen now and then. Why he had to have his breakfast egg in there I never found out. Perhaps to remind him that he was bottom of the pile? He was a strange boy but he could be sweet. I reckon he was about 15, but he was so small, he could have been ten. He hardly ever had a conversation with anyone in my hearing.

After my first week he came up to me one morning and said, 'Leave yer shoes out and I'll clean 'em.' I think Cook had told him to. Having your shoes cleaned was one of the few little perks you sometimes got as a live-in servant – as long as you weren't the lowest of the low like The Boots or the scullery maid. It was copying the big houses, really, where The Boots and the scullery maid and the lowest housemaid did all the drudgery for the upper servants: washing their clothes, making their breakfast and so on.

When The Boots said he'd clean my shoes, I think that was the first time I noticed anyone looking at me in an odd way. By that I mean he was giving me a look that little girls don't get but that young women do. I hadn't a clue what it meant at the time. It sort of dawned on me gradually as it does on most girls at some stage as they grow up. The Boots did it and eventually men I passed on the street did it now and then. It was just a bit of a special stare as they went by.

I didn't know much about the birds and the bees – well not in detail. But I tell you what, I was bloody good looking and I'm not surprised I had a few stares despite being a domestic!

Getting breakfast for The Kipper was a bit of a palaver. I was amazed at how much she wanted prepared for her each day. She always asked Cook to make kippers and porridge and toast and always tea and coffee. I'm sure it was a mark of status among the well off to throw away more than half the stuff we prepared. They did it just because they could, I suppose. So when I went to get the dishes back to clean them, if there was anything nice left I'd snaffle it off the plates on the way down the stairs.

As soon as The Kipper was in the dining room, where I'd got the fire going a couple of hours earlier, I went up to the bedrooms and started the fireplace business all over again. Same routine with the grates and carpets as I'd gone through in the reception rooms. Here I'd also make her ladyship's bed, tidy her clothes away and go round with my duster cleaning the surfaces – the tops as we called them – and then the floor on my hands and knees again.

To this day I haven't a clue where The Kipper's money came from. She could have been a bank robber for all I knew. I don't think she was as posh as she liked to make out. Mind you, I thought that about all my employers! I once found a box of postcards left out on the dressing table in her room and each picture was of a slightly fat looking woman without a stitch of clothing on! I didn't know what to make of it.

After a few days of this endless labour I thought I'd die if I didn't get a bit of time off. Wednesday came around eventually and I was free for half a day. Turns out I hadn't got a half-day in my first week because they'd given me my uniform, which I'd normally have to buy. That extra bit of work was my way of paying for the uniform. So it was two weeks before I had any real time to myself and at 15 years old, two weeks is a long time.

I was supposed to be let off at 1.00 pm. Then, at noon, I was told by Cook that she was sorry but till I finished my work I couldn't go out. It wasn't Cook's fault, it was just the system again. Once you'd worked as a domestic for a bit you realised that a lot of employers deliberately gave you more to do on your day off because really they resented you having any time off at all. On several occasions in my career as a domestic I heard the people I worked for talking to each other and saying things such as, 'Why on earth do they need to leave the house just to walk around the streets or sit in cafes? Most unreasonable.' Or words to that effect. They thought that we were so lucky to be working for them that we really shouldn't need to get away for a minute.

If I heard things like this, I was really upset. I was always so tired and fed up, but what could I do? It felt like they owned me body and soul. On that Wednesday I tried to work faster and eventually got the cleaning done by about three. Then off I went, but with no thought from anyone that I'd lost two hours of my precious half-day off.

It was lovely to be out in the air after more than ten days' cleaning and slaving. Like an idiot I did as I was told and went down to Kensington Gardens, which was further than Hyde Park. I walked by the Round Pond but I felt very lonely. And I didn't have any money so I couldn't have a cup of tea or an ice cream.

Then, out of nowhere and just as I was thinking about going back, a girl about my age sat down next to me and asked if I was new. It's funny, isn't it, but how did I know she meant new in the servant line? Well, I just did.

'Yes,' I said.

'Me too,' she said. 'Well that's a lie really,' she went on. 'I've been at Kensington – one of those huge houses down that way,' and she pointed in the opposite direction from the way I'd come. 'For the first month I kept getting lost and they had to send people to find me there were so many bloody back passages. But talk about airs and graces. You'd think the people I work for never blew their noses. Come to think of it they probably don't. If they wanted to I'd have to do it for them.' She laughed at the end of her little speech and said. 'I'd rather be in a factory, wouldn't you?'

'It's bloody hard work,' was all I could say.

'Are you a skivvy?' she then asked me.

'I'm a maid of all work.'

'You want to get out of that,' she said. 'Get into a bigger house where there's more servants – the more there are the less you have to do and the food's better and you might meet your husband.' She laughed again and in fact that's the thing I remember best about her – her laughs. We became great friends in a few minutes. In all the time I knew her any little joke or rude comment made her really laugh. Sometimes she got the giggles too and that would set me off.

Then she said: 'It's the jumped-up ones that's worst.' She then stopped and said, 'You don't know what I mean do you? I mean the ones that weren't born to it but made a bit of money and think they're as good as the best. Well they're not.'

Then she said, 'Where are you from?' I said Hoxton and she hadn't a clue where that was. She was from somewhere in the West Country. We each thought the other's accent was funny. Later on, when I knew her better, she told me that when she'd first come to London she couldn't understand her employers or any of the local cockneys. I really liked Mary from that first day and we agreed to meet every Wednesday on our afternoon off at the Round Pond. She said not to worry if I couldn't make it.

'They'll sometimes keep you there deliberately with extra work so it'll be so late it's not worth coming. Aren't they pigs?'

And then she really laughed. She was shocking sometimes. I thought I was cheeky, but when we parted that first time after she'd walked back some of the way to Park Lane with me, she shouted, 'Just remember they have to have a piss just like we do!'

It was a good point and from then on I always told myself that I was as good as any of them and that, just like Mary, the only real problem was that I hadn't been born rich.

People didn't hug and kiss much back when I was a girl. My family certainly didn't do it much, but every time I met Mary after that first meeting in the park I gave her a big hug. I think I had a bit of a crush on her. She said to me once, 'You want to watch it. You're a really good looking girl. The men'll be after you. You'd be much better to be ugly like me.' I nearly cried when she said that, and I told her she wasn't ugly at all – which she wasn't. She was what I think people call big boned and very dark – but she was such a laugh. When we walked round the park she'd sometimes say, 'Look at that one over there,' – pointing to a man – 'I wouldn't give you tuppence for ten minutes in the dark with him.'

One Wednesday a few months after we'd met, when the weather had warmed up a bit, Mary and I were walking around the park when I first saw someone having sex.

In those days you couldn't go to a hotel if you were poor. There weren't many hotels anyway and you'd always be asked if you were married. They'd also know straight away that you weren't hotel people by your clothes and the way you talked. Banks and hotels were as far off from us as China. So it was hard to even have sex before you were married. Far more girls *did* have sex in those days, both rich and poor, than you might imagine and they had clever ways to avoid pregnancy. The problem was that those clever ways didn't always work!

So there we were, walking arm in arm round the back of the

keeper's lodge in Hyde Park when I saw a naked bottom in the grass going up and down like a bleedin' sewing machine. I couldn't understand why a man would lie on the grass and do that with his trousers half way down his legs, but then it dawned on me. I saw there was a woman underneath him. We must have walked within 30 feet of them. Mary was laughing behind her hand, but they were so far gone they took no notice of us at all and they were really noisy. Mary said, 'Doesn't it give you the urge?' After that it wasn't Mary who was laughing it was me. I nearly choked but every time we met after that she'd say, 'Let's go and see if the arse is on show!'

Over the following months I gradually found out more about Mary. She was a workhouse girl, an orphan, and people normally only took on workhouse girls if they couldn't find anyone else. That was why she said she was ugly, I think, and why she tought she would never find a husband or get to be a better-paid servant. She felt she was marked after growing up in a workhouse. And in many ways she was because there was a huge prejudice against girls brought up on the parish.

It was awful for Mary to think so badly of herself when she was so alive and so much fun, but if I ever said I felt sorry for her she'd give me a shove and say, 'What are you on about? I'm all right. You can be my family.' And then she'd laugh and put her arm through mine and suggest we go and stick our tongues out at the soldiers in the park or buy a bun in Kensington to eat or a turnip to throw through someone's window.

She was always up to something and was always carefree and a bit of a rebel. But she'd clam up a bit when I asked her about her work and, strange as it sounds, I never found out where exactly she was. In some ways of course that wasn't so surprising. Servants didn't take their friends anywhere near where they worked on their day off. They wanted to get as far away from it as they could and for as long as they could. That's why any time near 10.00 pm on a weekday evening in any expensive part of London you'd see young girls running like mad along the roads trying to get back before the curfew and a scolding for being late. You weren't proud of where you worked.

But Mary made up for all the hard times I had at work. She'd talk to me about how I felt about things as no one had ever done before. And she always made me laugh. Always. She was so full of mad pranks. She'd flirt with complete strangers, particularly the soldiers who walked in the park down from the barracks at Knightsbridge. She brought out the cheeky side in me, too, which I loved because I'd been a bit overawed in my first days in my job. Once she shouted 'Oi, handsome, show us what you've got!' at a little group of soldiers hanging about near the Kensington High Street entrance to the park and they started to chase us! We ran out of the park and into a little side street and saw them run by without seeing us. We weren't scared at all, just bursting with laughter. 'What if they'd caught us?' I asked. 'We'd have kicked them where it hurts,' said Mary.

Mary completely changed the way I felt about work and I still look back and think she made the weeks and months fly by because she gave me something to look forward to every week.

I got back that first afternoon and evening off at about nine o'clock because it had been dark for a while by then and I'd been told I had to be back by ten at the latest. That was the rule and all servants were strictly watched to make sure they obeyed it. Employers thought they were doing you a favour by guarding your morals. What they really meant was they wanted to make sure you didn't have any fun.

There really was a feeling then that working people, particularly girls, couldn't be trusted to have fun. They'd get dissatisfied with their lot in life. They'd get bolshie or immoral. When I met my future husband he used to say that it was all down to the ruling classes getting in league with the church to tell poor people to knuckle under in this life so you'd get your reward in the next. He said it was a bloody con and I suppose he was right.

The old Kipper wasn't so bad about this kind of thing because I don't think she noticed so much and she led a strange life anyway. In later houses I always had to carry a brass can of hot water upstairs in the morning for the mistress and other family members to wash with. In The Kipper's house I was never asked to do it – well, not until her husband got back from wherever he'd been gallivanting, but that was later on.

I think she was one of those old-fashioned women who just hated washing. She covered herself in scent and makeup instead. This was a common solution at a time when washing every day wasn't a general habit.

There was a bath in the house. We had to heat the boiler – we called it the copper – first. But I think most of the time the old lady just couldn't be bothered.

I was allowed one bath a week. I was lucky. In big houses two or even three housemaids might have to use the same bath water one after another – can you believe that? But here I had my own water. It was never very hot but I loved it as we had no bath at home. I'd mostly only had a bit of a rub down before. Now I had my own four inches of water every Friday night at 9.30, which was roughly when I stopped working.

Chapter Thirteen

When it came to clothes and linen, most houses did their own washing – unless it was a big house. Then they'd send it out or maybe have a building attached to the main house that was made into a laundry.

Monday was the usual day. And that was my next surprise: the complications of wash day. In a big house Cook would never have got involved, but here we all had to muck in. So the sheets and linen napkins, everything, went in a big tub that was filled with water and soap.

Skinny little me then turned a cast iron handle which sort of agitated a paddle inside the barrel. It was like a primitive washing machine. My arm nearly fell off with the effort. Then we tipped the water out into a drain in the stone floor and filled up with clean water and started turning the handle again.

After that we put everything through a big old mangle that was fitted to the top of the great wooden barrel. It was murder getting sheets through that mangle. We needed a ruddy great navvy really to do it properly. I thought I'd get a bloody hernia, but The Boots helped and the two of us would swing and haul on that handle as if our lives depended on it.

But it was amazing how much of the water the mangle squeezed out, which was just as well because in that damp old basement it would otherwise have taken a month to dry the clothes from a single wash in winter. It was all right in summer but in winter we'd hang everything on a 'lazy Betty' – well, that's what we called it. When not in use it was pulled up to the kitchen ceiling. Then it was lowered again when we needed it. It had six narrow wooden poles running along side by side and held in a sort of cast iron frame at either end. You put the clothes over the poles and then hauled it up to the ceiling out of the way with ropes and pulleys. Since heat rises the clothes would usually dry in a day or two and then, if there was more to dry, the next lot would be hauled up. I don't think the process really took much dirt out of the clothes compared to modern washing.

After a few weeks I found I was making fewer mistakes. I'd got the hang of laying the table, cleaning the reception rooms each morning and laying and lighting the fires, helping with the meals, doing the bedrooms in the afternoon and getting the meals ready, especially in the evening, before finally washing up. The old Kipper, Mrs Williams, was still a mystery to me. She'd have her friends round for dinner or lunch most days and sometimes a lady friend of hers or a couple would stay overnight or for the weekend.

Some evenings they would play bridge and then the bloody bell would be endlessly tinkling and I'd have to go up maybe half a dozen times. She'd always ring if the fire needed more coal even though she was sitting six feet from the grate with a couple of burly blokes. It was all about show, you see. It was about showing who you were and who you could command. So the maid had to run up in her little black dress and cap and tip a new load of coal on the fire and then go out backwards.

I looked up at them now and then when I thought they weren't looking at me. Just glanced up as I turned away from the fire and they seemed so ordinary, so boring looking that it was hard to envy anything except their easy lives. One time when I had a quick look at them Mrs W caught my eye. Next morning Cook told me that The Kipper had asked her to tell me never to do it again. I was a bit upset by that because I'd barely looked at all, really. It was just a glance but I vowed I'd look at the floor rather than their ugly mugs after that.

When I finally asked Cook about Mr Williams and if he was dead she said. 'You shouldn't really ask about your employer. It's none of our concern what they do, but I can tell you he is a vicar. He goes off half the year or more and then comes back. But we don't ask where he goes and we don't want to know. Anyway, he'll be back soon and you'll have to look lively when he's around.'

The next humiliation, just when I'd got used to my freezing room and only having a few hours off each week, was that Mrs Williams spotted my swollen red raw hands. They'd got in a right mess from all the sand and soda and vinegar I'd been using every day. They hurt like hell and had scabs on them. They were so red you could have seen them glowing in the bloody dark. So Cook told me that when Mrs W had guests as I served lunch or cleared the tables I was to wear gloves.

I'd always thought of my hands as very pretty and it wasn't my fault they looked like big red cabbages now, but what could I do? No one seemed to have heard of protective gloves back then. There was no plastic of course so I suppose gloves would have been expensive and wouldn't have lasted if they'd been leather or cotton. Leather gloves would have been wrecked in a few days and no employer would have paid for them or allowed a servant to wear them anyway. So from then on I wore gloves to protect The Kipper from the sight of my raw hands. Then I took them off when it was time for scrubbing and cleaning

As this was my first job I didn't know that a lot of the things that went on would have been sniffed at by better-off people in bigger houses. But that's how it was then. The upper servants in big houses despised the lower servants – they were encouraged to despise them – and even the lowest housemaid in a big aristo-cratic house thought she was miles above the skivvy and maid of all work in a smaller house. People in grand houses thought that people with only a couple of servants or, God forbid, just one, were miles beneath them. You see this obsession with status? Servants in really big houses even thought their employer's status rubbed off on them and in a way it did. If only we'd realised that we were all just bloody slaves! With TV and a few hours' work a week, central heating and three meals a day, a prisoner in the Scrubs gets a better deal now than we did back then.

Chapter Fourteen

After we'd been meeting for about three or four months Mary told me that I should look about me for another situation – that's what we always called jobs. Sounds funny now to think we talked about finding 'a situation'. I think it made it sound less like drudgery!

I was really surprised when she said this; I'd never thought of such a quick change. I'd been home to Hoxton a couple of times on my days off and though I'd moaned a bit about the job my mum had just said, 'What did you expect?' She was also grateful for the money. My ten shillings a week seemed a fortune to me and I gave half to my mum. I think Mum would have thought I was mad to think about moving so soon and I said as much to Mary but she just laughed and said, 'Yer mum won't mind if you get paid more will she?' And of course that was true.

Payment of wages was another rigmarole that involved bowing and scraping by me and queenly nods from The Kipper. I was given my money by Mrs W each month in a really funny little ceremony. She'd ring the bell from the drawing room on the last Friday of the month. Cook would go up and collect her money and the money for Tommy The Boots – the poor lad only got about six shillings a week. Then she would ring for me.

Mrs W would be sitting with her back to the window behind a big mahogany desk. She'd look up at me and say something like, 'Cook tells me you are a hard worker,' or 'Cook tells me you were late on Wednesday,' or 'Cook tells me you broke a plate. That'll be sixpence off your wages.' Only then would she hand over the money.

Mary used to say that it broke their hearts to have to pay us at all. They thought so much of themselves that they couldn't understand why we didn't work for nothing, just for the joy of looking after such angels. Mary always came up with a screamer like that.

So when Mary said I could probably get an extra shilling or two if I went for a housemaid I began to think about it. She also explained that being a maid of all work was just about the worst job you could possibly have in service. Well, how was I supposed to have known that?

When I started to think about getting a new job I worried that I wouldn't get a good reference from Mrs W if I left after I'd been there for maybe only six months. In fact my six months were almost up by now. But Mary, who seemed to know absolutely everything about domestics, told me that servants moved around a lot and that a bad reference was often seen as just an employer's annoyance at the loss of a servant.

'Your best bet,' said Mary, 'is to get yourself down to Massey's in Baker Street.' I hadn't a clue what she was talking about. She quickly explained that Massey's was an agency where you just went along and asked if they had any jobs. They specialised in domestic service jobs. You told them what you'd done and they fixed you up with something. It was in their interest to find you something, she said, because servants were getting harder to find and Massey's didn't get paid if they didn't find places for people. 'Down at Massey's, you're in charge!' she used to say.

So I began to think about this and Mary and I talked about it a lot on our days off. When I asked her why she didn't move as well and that maybe we could be in two houses closer to each other she gave me a funny look and said, 'I'm a workhouse girl so it's not so easy. As soon as anyone hears that they make some excuse, but you'll be all right. You can tell them you've got a mum and a dad, even if they do live in Hoxton!' And off she went again chuckling to herself and giving me a nudge.

We had no thought of working in the same house. That wouldn't have been a good idea at all, even if it had been possible, because one of us might end up above the other in the hierarchy and it would be hard to be friends then.

There were three levels of servants, I realised. Workhouse kids were considered the scum, but they were cheap. City kids like me were next best. But best of all was a country girl. Employers liked girls from the country because they thought they worked harder, never complained, never asked for a pay rise and, best of all, never left. Bloody typical wasn't it? They wanted country girls because they could be treated even more like a machine than the rest of us!

But back to work. The weeks passed and it was late summer by now and all my happiest times were with Mary. Tommy The Boots was fun sometimes too and a right cheeky little elf but kind-hearted. He did my shoes for me beautifully every night. And I was lucky because in a big house if there'd been half a dozen servants, I'd have had to do all the servants' boots and shoes with him.

Then when I was all settled into my routine something big happened. Mr Kipper, the vicar himself, turned up and Mrs Williams started having her hot water carried up in a can! How I laughed about that.

Sometimes it had to be two cans and I heard her saying to Cook, 'It isn't hot enough some mornings Mrs James. Test it with your elbow. It really is most important. And I must have it at 7.30 sharp.'

You had to carry a towel draped over the can of water when you carried it up, and after you poured it into the wash bowl the towel had to be left covering it. When I left the bowl in the dressing room next to Mrs W's bedroom I had to check the soap was dry. That was really important, I was told. If it was wet, I had to dry it very carefully.

The vicar was terrible. Much more demanding than Mrs W. He would be in bed till nine and then start ringing the bell like a maniac. He'd start shouting if I didn't get up there with his shaving water straight away. Cook just used to turn her eyes up to heaven when he started.

Often he'd ring again ten minutes later and get me back up there with more water or complain that the first lot wasn't hot enough. He'd then eat a huge breakfast. Every day we'd make kidneys, kippers, porridge, bacon, eggs and tomatoes, enough for 20 people, and every day a lot of it was still thrown away. We weren't supposed to eat the leftovers, because the rich in those days thought it would spoil us for our place in life. It would make us get above ourselves, as they used to say. But sod that! Of course we used to eat it if we could. I remember scoffing some delicious bits of bacon on the back stairs. I could get them down me in the time it would take you to blink.

The Reverend and Mrs Kipper definitely thought it was better for us servants if we had plain food and not too much of it. All the other people I later worked for had pretty much the same idea.

There were new restrictions now the vicar was back in the house. 'He's the real boss,' Cook used to say. I was told I had to be back earlier than usual on my Wednesday half day and I was reminded again – and on several occasions – that no 'followers' were allowed. That is, no boyfriends. Cook told me that if the vicar glanced out the window and so much as saw me talking to a boy I'd be out.

Funny isn't it? The vicar was horrified we might sneak a kiss in the street but he didn't seem to mind much if we slept in freezing bedrooms and worked regular 12-hour days.

The no-followers rule was really more about pregnancy than anything. It was the big fear in those days. And of course it was instant dismissal if they found out you were pregnant. Mind you, even us rough working girls thought pregnancy would be a terrible scandal and we'd deserve to get the push. You almost always fell in with the general view of these things. But girls did get pregnant despite the consequences. We heard about it now and then on the servant grapevine which was based in and around the park and especially Speaker's Corner. The real reason a lot of girls got pregnant is that they had no idea about sex at all.

Some girls really didn't realise that sex was how babies were made. They just thought it was one of those slightly odd but nice things all men wanted to do. Some girls thought it was kissing that brought the babies along. We were such innocents. There were no books to tell us about these things and most mums and dads would rather have died than tell their children anything at all about the facts of life. But if an ordinary house was strict about its servants' morality imagine how much worse it was in a house run by a vicar!

After his huge breakfast the old vicar would read the papers while we slaved downstairs and in the bedrooms. Then he'd have an equally huge lunch and again we'd get tons of cooking stuff out and I'd have to spend the afternoon cleaning it, the kitchen and everything in the kitchen, sometimes including the walls.

Even the sinks we used for cleaning clothes and dishes had to be cleaned in a special way. Because they weren't glazed, they absorbed all the fat from the food and stank if you didn't scrub them regularly with soda.

Chapter Fifteen

I always spent my half-day off with Mary and we almost always spent some of our time, or most of it, talking about boys. Everyone wanted a soldier back then because of the uniform. If you were a servant girl and you met a boy in the park on your night off – we usually just walked round the park as we had no money – you'd never show him your hands as no boy wanted a girl in service. If I started talking to a boy in the park – and it happened more often than you might think – I always used to lie and say I worked in a shop, which was seen as really classy by domestics. We'd have thought that was a really big step up in the world!

We liked to flirt with the boys a bit just for a laugh. We didn't really want a steady boyfriend and I expect that, despite our pretence, they all knew we were servants really. I used to tell them whatever came into my head. It was the old East End patter coming out, I suppose, and I was really good at it. I loved spinning them a yarn. It all had to be done in the open of course, because we had no privacy. We had nowhere to go.

Boys would just walk up to you in the park and start a bit of banter. Mary would always say, 'We don't mind having a walk round the park with you and your friend but keep your hands to yerself.' And then we'd walk and flirt. Then they'd have to go back to wherever they worked or we would make an excuse and run off. If you really wanted to look smart you could give a guardsman a sixpence at Knightsbridge and he'd escort you round the park for half an hour. Isn't that funny – we had to pay them! We just loved the idea of being seen with a man in such a dazzling uniform. It was so exciting. Of course you couldn't get an officer but just a soldier was good enough for us.

I knew finally that it was time to get down to Massey's one day when I was cleaning the upstairs landing towards the end of that first year. The vicar had been back a while and the atmosphere in the house was definitely worse. Even Mrs W seemed to be afraid of the vicar's temper.

Anyway, there I was on the landing at the right time – that is, when the family should have been elsewhere – dusting away when I heard someone coming up the main stairs. I didn't have time to dodge into a bedroom or down the back stairs, which is what you were supposed to do, so I just turned to face the wall and, bearing in mind what had happened before when I'd got told off for glancing up, I made sure I kept my eyes on the little flowers on the wallpaper.

Next thing was I felt him stop behind me. I could tell it was the vicar. He just stopped and I thought 'Bloody hell. He's got stuck. Or he thinks I shouldn't be here.'

A bit of me wanted to giggle because I knew Mary would enjoy hearing all about this. Then I froze. I felt a hand on my bum. It wasn't just a light pat. He left his hand there quite gently for a bit, then he pushed and tried to get his fingers right between my legs.

I had my big apron on and my dress, as well as thick stockings – with very attractive thick pads sewn to the knees! – and a giant pair of bloomers made out of cotton as thick as sailcloth, so I knew he wasn't going to get very far. I wasn't shocked a bit. I didn't think of it as a sexual assault at the time. I didn't think of anything. I was just surprised.

I think he was disappointed and having shoved a bit more and done some odd, noisy breathing he stopped and I heard him go off down the corridor. I wasn't offended and outraged like a modern girl would be. I was just completely stumped. I thought what the bloody hell was that about? A bit of me thought he'd been checking to see if I'd wet myself or something! Then I thought I'd got muddled and maybe I shouldn't have been on the landing at that time and he was just trying to get past me?

I didn't say a word to Cook but when I saw Mary next I told her. She said, 'Dirty old bastard. He was after your pie he was.' She thought it was funny, but she was cross as well, I could tell.

No one would have dreamed of complaining about that sort of thing at that time and how could you complain to your employer when your employer was the problem? If I'd gone to Mrs W she'd have had to sack me. She could hardly chuck her husband out could she? I reckon she couldn't even tell him off, really, because she was scared of him.

And the truth is that most people assumed men were just acting according to their natures by doing that sort of thing. Old men had occasionally touched me when I was a kid. They just did it and everyone thought, 'Oh, that's just his way. He gets a bit lecherous.'

After that incident on the landing I was much more wary, but it was hard to keep out of his way. Oddly I don't think I was as bothered as Mary. She was quite protective towards me while I honestly thought it was just funny.

People had to learn to be bothered about sexual abuse. Back then no one ever talked about it and it happened one way and another all the time. Boys would grab you at a dance and try to kiss you if you left with them afterwards. If you kissed back they'd be all over you, grabbing you everywhere.

I remember once, later, during our alternate Sunday off, Mary and I found ourselves two very nice boys in the park. She wasn't that keen on hers, but I really liked mine. Well, we walked round for a bit and then went off to an area where there were a lot more trees and shrubs. We sat on the grass and just giggled and mucked about. But then suddenly my boy was kissing me like he was planning to eat the face off me. I quite liked it, I must admit, but I was horrified when he put his hand up my skirt.

I wasn't worried about being touched. What I was really worried about was that he'd notice the coarse canvas drawers I had on. They'd been stitched so many times I was crimson with shame. And another bit of me thought, 'Why is he touching me there? That's where I go to the toilet!'

The truth is I didn't really understand what I was supposed to be doing or what it was all for. Mary pretended she did but I think she was as muddled as I was, really. But then we were very young and we lived in an age when people matured much later and only found out about things, if at all, bit by bit from gossip.

We escaped from those boys by promising to meet them the next week – which we had absolutely no intention of doing. Quick as you like, Mary and I scarpered. She'd just sat and talked to her boy she told me, but we'd both had a good time.

I got a bit worried later that I might have been seen. But it was unlikely as Mr and Mrs W never went to the park as far as I knew, and they had no children, which was lucky for us. I say children because it was the teams of nannies in the park who might have told on me. People were interfering busybodies back then. They'd shop you for sixpence and to suck up to their employers and show that they were far more moral than the servant they'd just grassed up.

A few weeks later I met Mary in Baker Street and we went to Mrs Massey's. It was, as Mary had said, an employment agency strictly for domestic servants. People used to say it was much better to go to Massey's or one of the other agencies for a new job than to bother with newspaper advertisements, but I knew girls who did both. Newspapers were seen as a source of slightly dodgy jobs for some reason.

I was amazed at how busy it was at Massey's. Although I

94

didn't know it at the time, it was getting much harder to get domestics and to keep them. Girls were starting to realise that there was more to life than being someone else's slave. They were beginning to realise that, with a bit of education, they might be able to work in an office if they didn't fancy factory work or domestic service. There were definitely more opportunities than there had been 20 years earlier.

Anyway, Massey's was really busy when we got there – a bit like Smithfield market! There was a long desk with a row of chairs in front of it and in front of each chair a line of women. We picked a chair and joined the line behind it and waited as we slowly moved towards the front. When it was your turn you just popped your bum in the chair and talked to one of their staff about what you wanted.

There was a completely separate bit of Massey's which was much better got up. This was where the employers came. They even had their own front door completely separate from our way in. Mary and I used to say, 'Here we go again! They don't want to catch common!'

Our bit of the office was all drab wood and no ornaments. So even here there was an idea that if you worked you didn't need all the finer things. Thank God all that has gone.

So there we were with a load of other women all looking for new jobs. And looking back I realise how we all looked the same. The pressure to conform was huge then. You'd be amazed how desperate people were not to stick out in any way. Not like after the Second War and then the 1960s where it was completely the opposite. I loved it when I used to see boys with long hair and bright clothes. Why shouldn't we all dress up a bit? There was nothing good about the drab old stuff we used to wear. Though we had it better than our mothers, I must say. My skirt hem was half way up my calf by the late 1920s – wasn't I the saucy trollop!

Mary had told me to say I definitely didn't want to be a maid of all work or a tweenie – a tweenie worked with the housemaids in the morning and as a kitchen maid in the afternoons.

So when it was my turn I sat down and said I wanted to be a housemaid. That would at least get me out of the hard jobs in the kitchen that ruined your hands.

The woman on the other side of the counter asked what experience I had. I exaggerated a bit to make it sound like I did less in the kitchen and more in the house, because Mary had told me that housemaid's work was easy and there were lots of perks.

There and then the woman I saw offered me lots of jobs – third housemaid in a big house out in Hertfordshire, under housemaid in a house in Nottinghamshire and several in London. She told me I'd have to go for an interview, but that it would probably be all right. I thought, I'm not bloody going out in the countryside miles from anywhere. I'd have even less to do in my free time, and besides I'd already agreed with Mary that I'd try to get something close to the park so we could still meet. Eventually I said I'd try for a job as third housemaid in a big house just off Park Lane. She asked if I had references, I obviously looked blank so she said I'd have to ask my present employer for a reference. I was worried about that because I thought she won't like me leaving so she might get her own back by not giving me a reference.

The main thing about agencies such as Massey's was that they didn't really mind what sort of reference you had. They always said references were important, but the truth is that they were desperate to get you a job. They loved it the more often you came back to them to change jobs, because every time they found a place for someone they got paid a fee. I was told that when they started up they made the servants pay, but by the time I went there the employer had to pay their fee because we were getting more valuable and harder to find.

I had my interview in the big Park Lane house the following week and they offered me the job there and then, subject to references.

My interview was with the housekeeper. 'You're on trial,

mind. If you don't suit you're out!' That's what they all said in the 1920s and 1930s. And this one looked liked she'd murder you in a minute. Tall and thin, with a hard face more like a man's and with huge hands like a navvy. As I got to know her I realised she could be terrifying one minute and nice as you please the next. I think she played at being harder than she really was because she was permanently terrified that she'd get into trouble if any of her staff didn't do their jobs properly. That's why she got in a state when a plate was broken or any of the ladies or gentlemen said that the least thing wasn't quite right.

Back at my old place I waited a few days before telling Cook I was leaving. She'd seen a lot come and go and was used to it, I suppose, and I'd been there less than a year so she didn't make a fuss.

'You'd better go up after dining room breakfast and tell Mrs W,' she said. 'Will she be angry?' I asked.

'Don't worry,' said Cook. 'She knows people never stay these days.'

I'd been hoping she'd tell the old lady for me, but this was clearly one of the very few times when the hierarchy changed. I'm for it now, I thought.

I was ready to go up to Mrs W the next morning when the bell rang and Cook told me it was time. It had all been prearranged, I suppose, and Cook had probably already spoken to Mrs W.

Mrs W met me in the hall – the hall I'd first seen with my mum nearly a year earlier – and beckoned me into the glass-house. She sat at a cane desk and looked straight at me for a long time, which was very uncomfortable. Then she just said, 'I'll have to deduct two shillings from your final pay for breakages and carelessness.'

I didn't have the courage to say that I hadn't broken a thing. When I told Cook she was furious and said the old bitch always does that or something like it.

I left at the end of the month and of course I had to give my uniform back. That was my first big shock at the new house. My wages were better – they'd gone up four shillings a month – but I had to buy my own uniform. I was allowed a half-day off each week as I'd had with Mrs W, but I was also allowed every other Sunday off.

I thought I was going up in the world, what with Mary being excited for me and saying, 'No more bloody spud peeling for you!' But though I didn't yet know it, I was really only going from the frying pan into the fire.

Chapter Sixteen

I went home to Hoxton after the end of my time with Mrs W and before I started the new job. My mum said she'd buy me the uniform. We walked to the West End to a shop that sold maids' uniforms. How different that journey was compared to the same journey on my first morning at work! I felt like a woman of the world this time. My mum seemed somehow smaller and less experienced than me.

There were quite a few servants' outfitters – hardly surprising when you think of the millions of women and girls employed in the trade.

When I told the shopkeeper what I needed they asked me what colour I wanted. Well, I'd never heard of that before. I thought they'd all be the same colours.

In the end I bought two dresses; a blue one for the morning and black for the afternoon, and several aprons. The woman in the shop said she'd change them if they were wrong. Then it was home to Hoxton for a night before starting my new job on the Monday.

Again I was to live in, and this was a blessing really because I realised I'd got out of the habit of sharing a bed. I was bloody uncomfortable at home and hardly got any sleep. A few days later I got the bus part of the way in the morning with my smart new uniform, money in my pocket and my few spare things in my bag.

As I went along I remember thinking it was a bit of a liberty getting me to pay for my own uniform, but Mary and the others told me it was the usual thing. I thought it was a terrible waste of six shillings on stuff I only had to wear to be someone else's slave.

I knew the ropes now, so when I got to the new house I went round the back. Well, it was actually more the side of the house and, sure enough, I saw the usual tradesmen sign and the steps down. The house is long gone. It was a big old Georgian thing that seemed to have more rooms under the pavement than above it. It had huge windows and two curved bays with even bigger windows that came almost down to the floor. They had to get men in to clean them every now and then because they were so heavy we couldn't even open them!

I don't know if the house was bombed in the Second War or demolished to make way for a hotel or something. It was stone-flagged in the basement like houses usually were then. There was no carpet or rug anywhere in the back part of the house where the servants lived. It was also much bigger than my first house – maybe twice the size. I'd like to tell you what it was all like but I was only ever allowed to see certain bits of it – the bits I cleaned. That was another mad rule: you were sacked if you were ever seen in a part of the house you were not responsible for cleaning. In Mrs W's house I'd pretty much cleaned everywhere at one time or another. But not any more.

Life was far more complicated now because there were a lot more servants. Not as many as in a really big house where there might have been four or five housemaids, several footmen and half a dozen kitchen staff as well as gardeners and odd-job men. But still there were three housemaids and I was the junior. I shared a room right at the top of the house with Gertie, one of the housemaids. There was also a butler and a footman, a kitchen maid and a scullery maid, cook, a lady's maid, parlour maid and a laundry maid.

* * *

The truth is that no two houses were the same in those days. It all depended. If there was no boots then the scullery maid polished all the shoes including the servants' shoes. She also did the worst of the washing up and cleaning in the kitchen. If there was a boots then the scullery maid only did kitchen duties, mostly cleaning. In my new house the kitchen maid and the scullery maid didn't get on well. The kitchen maid was always worried she'd get asked to do something that was really the scullery maid's job. And the poor scullery maid, who became a sort of friend of mine – but I'll tell you about that later – was upset by the way the kitchen maid, and everyone else for that matter, looked down on her. Ridiculous really – we were all in the gutter squabbling over scraps of nothing.

While the kitchen maid and the scullery maid helped produce breakfast and lunch and dinner, as well as keeping the kitchen clean, I started on my new career as a sort of human Hoover. Housemaids were each given a wooden box with a hinged top and filled with cleaning kit: cloths, emery paper, some sort of homemade polish, a hearth brush and a carpet brush.

When we were at work we set off up the stairs as a strictly regulated team, only ever using, of course, the back stairs.

We used to emerge on the ground floor where we were supposed to clean the breakfast room, drawing room and sitting room – there were actually two large sitting rooms – the smoking room, library and study. We were supposed to do all this before the family came down.

I'd only met the housekeeper and other staff on that first day and I never really found out who our employers were or what they did, which may seem amazing to anyone born half a century later than me. We were servants so it was none of our business. We were not allowed to ask and it was absolutely normal never to meet your employer unless you were one of the gentry servants, the parlour maid or lady's maid. In really big houses the back-of-house servants hardly had anything to do with the front-of-house servants and if you did happen across one of them and spoke to him or her – or if you even looked them in the eye – you'd be in trouble. It was worse than the caste system in India.

Technically the housemaids were front of house in the sense that they got a look at the best rooms while they cleaned them, but they had to do it in a way that made sure they never saw the family. The head housemaid wasn't a bad old stick but she took a real pride in her work and you knew you couldn't say a word against your employer if she was around. She was a really old-fashioned sort of domestic who idolised the gentry and thought she'd been born with a silver spoon, just because she was allowed to work for them. This seemed a mad idea to me even then, but she hated the idea of servants' back-chat, as she called it.

'You young girls are too full of yourselves,' she used to say. I think she could sense that things were changing and that rather than bowing and scraping to our betters we really wanted to stick our tongues out at them, and she didn't like it.

So there we were, three housemaids ready for action. We got to the ground floor about 6.00 am, I should think – well before the family came down. The lowest housemaid – that was me – had to lay the fire in our first room, which was the drawing room. The head housemaid quickly explained what I had to do and I got on with it. I threw old used tea leaves in on the ashes. That was new to me.

It was done to try to stop the ash floating around the room and leaving dust everywhere on the tops – the mantelpieces, the pictures, frames, ornaments and tables. If I kicked up dust the head housemaid had more to do so I wouldn't be popular.

So I put a special sheet down, cleared out the ash as carefully as I could, leaving the bigger bits of clinker as I'd been taught to do. I then started to polish the marble fireplace which was bloody enormous and the bars of the grate. I soon had the bars gleaming silver.

Then I went to help the second housemaid to clean the carpet. She told me to lift the edges of the big rug – a massive carpet, at least 20 feet long. On our knees we went slowly round combing out the fringes! They had to be combed out perfectly straight. If they were messy at all you'd get it in the neck from the head housemaid later on when someone in the family complained, which they often did.

The head housemaid, who was called Hilda even though her name was Margaret (I never got to the bottom of that one!), hated the idea of anything being out of place. She watched us like her life depended on it. As we worked Hilda dusted the table tops, the ornaments, photographs and that sort of thing. There were loads of tables in that house and about six in the drawing room alone, and they were covered with picture frames, china ornaments and silver trinkets and boxes.

Only the head housemaid was allowed to do the tops because she was assumed to be experienced enough not to drop or break anything. A rough girl from Hoxton couldn't be expected to handle porcelain and pictures! As Hilda dusted the tops she might say, 'Rose, you're making too much dust. Tomorrow use more tea leaves and work more carefully.' Or she might say, 'That's lovely, Rose. You can be proud of that.'

We did the whole of that 20-foot-long rug on our knees every day using small brushes and pans. We'd all heard of Hoovers but no one had seen one.

As we were getting towards the end of our work in that room the head housemaid, who'd been hovering near the door, suddenly said we had to go out. So we trooped out – the head housemaid first, second housemaid next and me last holding the door. What was so funny was that we knew we had to be quick but the head housemaid still waited for me to cross the room to the door and open it rather than speed things up by opening it herself. That just wasn't done. We nipped through the door on to the servants' staircase. Once the door was closed the head housemaid put her fingers to her lips and listened. She was so attuned to the sounds in the house that she had heard one of the bedroom doors opening upstairs while we were working. Assuming that one of the family members might be coming down earlier than normal, she made us all disappear until the coast was clear.

She really did have an uncanny knack for knowing when someone was coming. After a few minutes we went out again and headed for the sitting room as the drawing room was now finished.

I was supposed to open the sitting room door and let the others in first. That was always the rule and though I'd remembered at the drawing room door earlier, I forgot this time. I just opened the sitting room door and went in first myself. Hilda was momentarily furious with me. 'Never do that again,' she said while standing right in front of me wagging her finger up and down in my face.

We carried out the same procedure in the first and second sitting rooms – actually called the blue sitting room and the yellow sitting room – with me on my knees doing the fireplace and then helping Gertie, the second housemaid, with the carpets and the floor around the carpets.

Cleaning a massive carpet with a small hand brush and a little dustpan is something everyone should try just once – but to be realistic you have to do it in your stockings which means your knees will be killing you. While you're at it you have to work out a way to do the cleaning without missing a bit, because your work will be checked. I used to imagine a square yard starting from one corner and try to do it bit by bit left to right a square foot at a time. I heard from Gertie that even if the head housemaid didn't check everything when we'd finished, the butler would sometimes send word down that the colonel or his wife had noticed a bit of dust somewhere. That was the most dust-free house in history I reckon – but to keep us at it they invented little complaints.

Chapter Seventeen

It was about this time that I really began to question the world I was in, rather than just feeling a bit rebellious and taking the mickey now and then. The housekeeper and head housemaid, as I've said, were steeped in the old way of looking at service. By this I mean they admired the people we worked for and would have done anything for them. They thought they were lucky to be working in this big house with a ton of silver plate and cutlery in the basement. Even Gertie the second housemaid used to say, 'You wouldn't get me in a factory . . . all that noise and foul language.'

Sometimes when we had an hour off in the afternoon, usually between dining room lunch – that meant lunch for the family – and tea for us, we'd sit and talk in our room. I could never convince Gertie that the people who employed us thought of us as less than human. She just wouldn't accept it. She couldn't see it at all. The fact that we didn't finish most days till ten in the evening didn't seem a problem to her or the other housemaids at all. 'You're one of those Bolsheviks,' Gertie used to say with a smile. I hadn't a clue what she meant, though of course I found out later.

Gertie had been a housemaid for 15 years and had risen only one rung up the ladder, but she seemed to think that was fine. Working-class girls weren't brought up to be ambitious and it was all Buggins' turn back then. If the first housemaid died or left you might get the job but not otherwise. And our first housemaid – old finger-wagger – was never going to leave. Gertie and Hilda didn't seem to mind about having so little time off or being woken at night, or sometimes not being allowed to leave for their half-day holiday till their work was done. They didn't mind about all this because they thought a bit of class would rub off on them. And of course none of it rubbed off. We were all still servants and all we could do to make ourselves feel better was say, 'At least we don't work in a factory where you could lose a hand in a machine.' I used to say to Gertie that if a bit of the family's class did rub off on us and the family noticed – which they never would – they'd just laugh at us aping our betters. But Gertie was deaf to all my arguments, bless her.

Chapter Eighteen

One of the funniest moments in the Park Lane house came about because, when there were visitors, we lowly house-maids sometimes had to maid for any woman who didn't turn up with her own lady's maid. Most really well-off women at that time had a lady's maid. There was one in the Park Lane house but I never laid eyes on her in all the years I worked there. She was front of house and slept in the room next to her mistress. Like all ladies' maids she did her mistress's hair, laid out her clothes, mended them, all that sort of thing. She did everything except go to the toilet for her. I used to joke with Mary and ask if ladies' maids received any training for wiping their mistresses' bottoms. Mary used to screech with laughter at that.

But to be a lady's maid you had to be quite posh or at least a lot posher than we were. However long you worked as a house-maid you could never, ever move up to lady's maid or governess. Ladies' maids and governesses were always well educated. They were middle class or middle-class-fallen-on-hard-times, or educated above their station in life. But we maided quite a few women who came to stay, just for a day or two at a time – a bit like a temporary promotion with no more money attached. I remember I maided one middle-aged woman, a friend of the master, who stayed for a couple of weeks in my first winter.

This was how it worked.

You had to go up to their room when they arrived, curtsey and say, 'May I unpack for you now, Madam?' If they were obviously young and unmarried you referred to them as 'Miss'.

There was a strict order here, too. The first housemaid was given anyone with a title or who was married. The second and third housemaids – I was the third, remember – maided single women, daughters or anyone further down the ranking for any reason. A divorced woman wouldn't get the first housemaid unless she was really aristocratic. If you were the King's mistress you would still get the first housemaid because royals could do no wrong, though in practice, of course, she'd have enough money to have her own lady's maid.

I remember going up the back stairs to meet the first woman I had to maid for. She seemed all right. She was a short woman, about 40 years old I should think, good looking and very well dressed. I knocked, went in and curtseyed. Before I could say a word she glanced at me and said, 'Put out my cream dress for this evening and get my bath ready, would you?'

It went without saying that I should open her three suitcases and hang all her clothes in the wardrobe or put them in the chest of drawers. We used to put our clothes on a chair or on the floor when I was at home. So lucky I'd had it carefully explained.

While I was hanging the clothes she went into her adjoining sitting room and I emptied her bag. Now you'll never believe this but she had a sex aid in her bag. She must have known I'd find it. I didn't know it was a sex aid at the time but I found out later. A lot of magazines used to advertise them at that time. The word sex was never mentioned. They were called tension relievers or something like that, with no hint they had anything to do with sex. Do you know, a lot of women who bought and used them probably didn't think they had anything to do with sex anyway!

Sex for well-off women was only to have babies. You were not supposed to enjoy sex even with your husband in those days. In the late 1930s a friend of mine went to her doctor to ask if there was anything wrong because she didn't enjoy sex with her husband. The doctor said, 'Do you want people to think you are a prostitute?' Loads of people thought that only prostitutes liked sex.

Anyway these tension relievers were for posh women who got sexually frustrated but thought it was disgusting to get their husbands to sort it out for them, so they bought a little device to do it themselves. It was an old-fashioned vibrator!

How I laughed when I found out about that. But the fact that she let me empty her bag, knowing it was in there plain as anything, just shows that as far as she was concerned I was a servant so it didn't matter what I saw or thought. We were coached to hear and see nothing. Any gossip from below stairs would never reach anyone who mattered.

After I'd put her little device in a drawer I put her underwear away. I was amazed how much of it she had and it was all silk. I'd never seen such stuff before and can still remember running my hands over it and thinking how lovely it was.

I never rose to be a proper lady's maid – as I say, you had to be posher than I was for that. But I knew what they had to do. And but for the money, which would have been tempting, I don't think I'd have liked to do it. It might easily take your mistress an hour or an hour and a half to get dressed if she was going somewhere special. You'd have to help her put on pantalettes, camisoles, underskirts, overskirts, a chemise and gawd knows what else. Ladies' maids had to be really good at sewing, too, because without elastic and with the fashion in the 1930s for tight bodices you might have to sew madam into part of her clothing for the evening and then unpick her afterwards! And you had to sleep nearby in case the poor diddums needed something in the night.

Then there was the business of gloves and hats. She might have 50 of each and you'd have to fetch and carry them back and forth from the cupboard till she found something she liked. It could take forever. No, I was content to do just the occasional bit of maiding.

When I was maiding Mrs Charles, the woman with the vibrator, one of my duties was to fill her bath at night and in the morning. I'll give her that much – she washed a lot! They still didn't have running water to every room in the house and grand people often thought that bathrooms were beneath them, anyway. You'd often hear well-off people with lots of servants saying, 'We could install a bathroom for the servants, but it wouldn't be right for us or our guests.'

So for the next hour I carried hot water up from the kitchen one big brass can at a time, while Mrs Charles sat in the sitting room reading the paper and smoking a cigarette. I can't remember how long it took to fill the bath half full but it was a long time – maybe 20 or 30 cans hauled up the stairs over the space of about half an hour.

The bath had a sort of half hood at one end and it was set up always in front of the fire. When it had enough water in it I had to put the towels, three of them, on a wooden rail in front of the fire. When I meekly said to Mrs Charles, 'Your bath is ready, Madam,' she ignored me so I just thought, well she hasn't heard me, so I knocked on the door between the two rooms, which was open, and repeated it with my head sort of leaning through the door. Without turning round she just said, 'Do you mind not interrupting me. Just wait there till I am ready.' So I stood there feeling, to tell you the truth, as if I'd been slapped.

Most servants just blushed and resolved to be better when these sorts of things happened, but I was starting to get angry and resentful. This was a bad thing for a servant because it made life harder for you, but I was really beginning to hate the fact that pretty much everything was designed to put you in your place and remind you to stay there. I was lucky because things were gradually moving in the servant's favour as the world changed. Fifty years earlier I wouldn't have dreamed of being angry but the Labour Party was getting more powerful by now, along with the trade unions, and I remembered thinking, in 1926, that the general strikers were right and the bosses were wrong.

Chapter Nineteen

An example of servants being treated badly happened a few weeks later in this same house. We'd been told that we were only allowed to walk in the garden if the family was out and even then we were not allowed to whistle or sing or shout or run or be frivolous in any way. The rule about not running or singing was printed on a big notice on the inside of the door from the servants' part of the house that opened on to the steps going down to the garden, so you could never say you didn't know or that you'd forgotten.

I had an hour off one Saturday afternoon, something I'd never enjoyed in my first house, and the family was out. So I decided I would just sit in the fresh air on a bench that stood against the wall and caught the sun. I said hello to the gardener, who was an old man – maybe 60 or more. I didn't know him well, as housemaids were only ever allowed to talk to other housemaids and maybe occasionally the kitchen or scullery maid.

So I said hello and he nodded and smiled. I sat on the bench. I must have been there for 20 minutes when down the steps from above – from the family's part of the house – ran a boy of about 12 years. I think he was a distant relative of the family. Before I could retreat into the house so he didn't see me I saw him march up to the gardener and say in the angriest fashion you can imagine, 'How dare you move my ball? I deliberately left it on the bottom of the steps and you have moved it!'

The poor old gardener went red in the face and started to apologise, but the boy interrupted him and said, 'I don't want to hear your excuses. If it happens again you will be in serious trouble.'

And with that he walked off and back up the stairs into the house. For a mere boy to humiliate an elderly man like that seemed to me more than anything to show what a rotten system it was.

I'm not saying servants were always treated like this. In really big houses owned by the aristocracy it was sometimes a bit better but you would still hear stories all the time about the callousness of employers. Years after I left service I was chatting to a friend who'd also been a domestic. She told me how all the maids had been given a present one Christmas of some plain dress material. That was nice enough but all the maids were also given strict instructions by the lady of the house that they were to have the material made up into a work dress! They were nice sometimes but almost always with strings attached.

At the Park Lane house there were strings attached to pretty much everything. We were told we had to go to church on Sundays as a condition of our employment and I remember we were also told to dress as plainly as possible when we went and to sit according to rank: cook and butler closest to the front, followed by the housekeeper, footman and housemaids, with the scullery maid at the back.

What were the people we worked for thinking when the Bible reading declared that we were all alike in the sight of God? Didn't it make them feel even slightly guilty about the way they treated us? Well, I doubt it. The truth is that they just paid lip service to all that Christian stuff. I soon saw through it. The church was just another way to make you accept your lot. The rich man in his castle, the poor man at the gate – or half a mile away from the gate! It was just like the Salvation Army in the East End. They'd feed the poor but only after they'd sung endless hymns and been subjected to the sort of sermon that was so boring you'd have happily cut your own head off to avoid having to listen to it.

There were some lighter moments in the Park Lane house. I remember laughing till I nearly fell over when the butler told me that the best way to get the silver to really shine was to spit on it – and so that's what he used to do. He'd use a bit of polish as well but spit was used to get that fine gleam. Every time I was put down or told to cover up my 'unsightly' hands – that was the phrase someone once used – I'd think of the family eating their roast beef with knives and forks the butler had cleaned with spit.

Back in Mrs Charles's bedroom I was still standing there ten minutes after I'd been told off for interrupting. Then she appeared through the door and said, 'That will be all.' I did a little curtsey and disappeared. Once she'd had her bath I had to go back up with another housemaid and we'd carry the bath down the back stairs to empty it. Imagine if half a dozen women were staying. We had to do all their baths as well as the regular family baths. How we longed to be given the job maiding the smelly ones who never had a bath! And don't forget we had all our regular duties still to do when we were maiding visitors.

Chapter Twenty

What skinflints the rich were in those days! We were under strict instructions to collect any bits of soap or stubs of candles and re-use them. And any old disgusting bits of food – potato peelings, leftovers that were days old, all of it would go in a soup.

It was the same with brown paper and newspapers. If we found any grease spots or food stains on the reception room carpets or bedroom carpets – and you were bound to find a few, especially in the dining room – you had to go down to the kitchen to a special drawer and find some special thick brown paper kept for the purpose of stain removal.

You spread a sheet of paper on the stain and then went off to get a hot iron. We had a cast iron stove about five feet high in the basement that had ledges all the way around. You put your iron on a ledge and left it for 20 minutes or longer. Once you had your brown paper on the floor you nipped back down the stairs, grabbed a nice hot iron and then had to run back up the stairs as fast as possible before it got cold. You rushed in and immediately applied it to the brown paper to try to move the grease from the carpet to the paper. It worked reasonably well but never got all the grease out.

When you'd finished getting the stains out with the paper you went back downstairs and ironed the bloody brown paper before putting it back in its special drawer.

It was the same with napkins and sheets. They all had to be washed, ironed, folded and put away every week. They also had to be folded with the embroidered family initials showing in a corner.

Most people have heard about ironing newspapers. It's one of those stories you read all the time about what servants had to do. But few people realise that we ironed the papers not just once but several times a day. When they were delivered, and before they'd even been looked at, we gave them a once over. Then we ironed the stupid things again after the family had finished reading them over breakfast.

After family lunch, when they either went out or sat in the drawing room, we would clear the lunch things, tidy up and then iron those effing papers a third time. It was a bit of a nightmare, but not so much of a nightmare as the poor scullery maid's job in this house.

Edie had to do all the shoes and boots every day – about ten pairs on average, I would think. She had to polish the uppers and the soles because they were checked, not every day but sort of randomly so she was always on edge about it. One day I heard a funny noise in the kitchen when Cook was out and I found Edie crying in the cubbyhole in the basement where she often worked. She was the lowest paid in the house I think and treated pretty offhand by both the servants and the family – although the family would be no more likely to catch sight of her than the Duke of Edinburgh would be to catch sight of a saucepan.

When I opened the cubbyhole door and peeped in Edie was sitting on the floor covered in boot polish. Straight away she tried to stop crying, probably thinking she was going to get a scolding – but who the hell was I to give anyone a scolding?

I crouched down by her and asked what was wrong. She could only just speak through the gasps and sobs, but she said she'd been home on her day off and her mother had been horrible to her for some reason. She had got it into her head that her mother didn't want her back there at all. I had a piece of chocolate in my room so I ran up the back stairs to fetch it and I told her not to worry. When I offered her the chocolate she wouldn't take it for ages. When I finally persuaded her she suddenly asked me if I'd be her friend.

I nearly burst into tears when she said that. It was somehow heart-wrenching. I think it felt so bad because it was so rare for anyone to show their feelings at all back then. No one talked about it being good to show how you felt. It was really frowned on. And there was another problem.

Much as I liked Edie and felt so sorry for her, I wasn't really allowed to be her friend. It wasn't a rule that was written down, it just wasn't done. Housemaids in a big house didn't make friends with scullery maids in the same way that they didn't make friends with the housekeeper or the butler.

But I thought I must do my best, so I said I would look out for her and that if we had the same afternoon off she should come and meet my friend Mary. I gave her a hug and, thinking back all those years, all I can recall was that she was shaking and thin as a reed, all bone and sort of too narrow. I told her she'd soon get a bit more money and a better job and might meet a handsome footman. She smiled at that. She was a lovely girl but too timid for a tough kitchen. She'd come up from the country and could only read and write a little. I've never forgotten her. She did come out a few times with Mary and me, but she was afraid she'd get into trouble so she stopped after a bit.

One of the maids' jobs in this house was to mend the linen – as if we didn't have enough to do already. You'd think people as rich as they were would have been a little less penny-pinching, but like many people with a lot of money they were tight-fisted when it came to domestic things.

Every week when the linen came back from the laundry we had to check it carefully for tears and worn patches. I'm talking about the bed linen; we washed all the smaller stuff in the house. The point is there was always something that needed repairing. The sheets wore thin in the middle and then we would cut them in half down the centre and sew the outside edges together so that the thin middle was now on the outside.

This made the sheets last twice as long, but just try to imagine sewing together two long pieces of sheet. The job had to be done well and invisibly so tiny stitches were needed. There were probably at least a couple of thousand stitches needed to complete a single sheet. The second housemaid tended to do the sheets, while the first housemaid did the table linen. I got the lovely job of darning the family's bloody underwear – what a disgusting job that was. People didn't wear big knickers then – they wore bloody enormous ones. The men too.

When I sat there sewing the arse of their drawers up I used to think how funny it was that they saw nothing wrong with a young girl like me mending their underwear while at the same time we were told that we had to be very careful when maiding female visitors that their clothes were never visible. This meant not just their knickers, but all their clothes. And the reason was that one of the men servants might have to come into the mistress's room or a female guest's room to fix or open a window and might see intimate items of clothing left lying on a bed. Now that couldn't be tolerated could it? Imagine the scandal. Footman sees lady's scarf and gloves and she is ruined and can no longer go into society. That's not far off how people used to think. If you put out evening wear for someone you were maiding you did leave it on the bed but then you covered it with a special cloth until it was ready to put on.

Chapter Twenty-One

You might read that some girls loved being in service, because it meant they were in aristocratic houses and learned how to value nice things and to improve the way they spoke. It's probably true that a few did enjoy this kind of thing, but their efforts to improve themselves were always seen as either pathetic or alarming by the families they worked for. I had an example of this myself. I used to hear the odd bit of French being spoken – usually when visitors or the family didn't want the maid to understand what they were saying. All the toffs in those days had French governesses to make sure they spoke French like natives by the time they went to school. It didn't matter much to me as I heard lots of good stuff to tell Mary anyway as the family often forgot we were there and carried on speaking in English. Then, a few years later on a bit of a whim, I thought why shouldn't I have a few French lessons? I'd started reading by borrowing books from the local library. I could have been sacked if the family had found out and didn't approve of the sort of books I was reading.

I'd tried a bit of Shakespeare and Dickens, G.K. Chesterton, Kipling and a few others, and thought I wasn't doing so badly for a girl from the slums. And that's where the French came in. I got really brave and went to a place in Oxford Street that taught French. 'Young ladies and gentlemen taught the most elegant French at very reasonable rates,' it said on the door. I should have known what was likely to happen from that reference to 'ladies and gentlemen', but I'd walked a fair bit to get there and thought, in for a penny . . .

I went in and sat in a small waiting room with a lovely painting of the south of France on the wall and I remember the smell of violets. After about ten minutes a young woman came through a door and I saw straight away how her face dropped a bit when she saw me. As soon as I said what I wanted she sort of smiled grimly and said she was sorry but they were full up and couldn't take any more pupils. She then turned on her heel and disappeared through the same door she'd just come in.

I was really hurt because I knew what had made her react like that. But what could I do? I had the money but she didn't want to teach me at any price.

It was obvious I was a servant and when I opened my mouth it was even more obvious I was no lady! That was the sort of thing that made you develop a tough skin. Without it you got so much emotional bruising, so many setbacks and snubs that you could easily go under. A lot of servant girls killed themselves and not just because they were pregnant.

But I got over it. It was a humiliation and it was a typical reaction if you tried to improve yourself, but I never gave up. I tried to teach myself a bit of French using books from the library and though I never learned much I learned a bit. I always thought French with a good strong East End accent probably sounded lovely!

I stayed for seven years with the colonel – that's what we called the master – and in all that time none of the staff left. This was despite the fact that a lot of servants did start moving far more often, particularly after 1930. You have to remember that some domestic servants worried that if they moved things might be worse and older servants tended to move less anyway. They got stuck in their ways.

In all those years in the colonel's house I never met him and I hardly ever laid eyes on him – except a couple of times when I saw the chauffeur drive round to the gravel area at the front of the house to pick up an elderly man.

The chauffeur had been with the family since the 1880s. More than 50 years, which seemed to us girls an amazing thing. He was very old-fashioned, too, and still wore what looked like livery to me: a black suit with a bit of gold braid and a black tie. I never saw him out of that suit. He lived in a tiny mews house nearby with the car kept in the old stable below his bedroom and kitchen. Once the head housemaid sent me to his house after the phone stopped working. The phone was connected only to a few other big houses where they had friends – and to the chauffeur's house. You see, there was only a limited general phone network then because so few people had them.

I found the house, which had what looked like barn doors downstairs and no windows. The two small windows were upstairs. I pulled on a wire bell pull and waited. A few minutes later one of the big double doors began to open and the whiskery old chauffeur peeped out.

He touched his hat to me – something no one else had ever done – and asked me if I wanted a cup of tea. I said I had to get back to the house but could he take the car up as the master wanted to go out. He nodded and then started to talk to me, which was a real surprise. Older servants rarely passed the time of day with us young ones.

He said: 'I suppose you like these motorcars?'

I said I hadn't thought about it much.

'Come and have a look,' he said, so I did. He swung the big doors open and there was this huge gleaming car. 'She's a bloody brute,' he said. I couldn't think of a thing to say I just stood there in my cap and apron probably looking very stupid. Then I looked around the stable while he stared at the car and grumbled. I realised that the room which took up the whole of the ground floor of the house was still stacked with bales of hay at the back and hanging up was all the gear for a carriage. The carriage itself was over against the wall, leaving just enough room for the car to get in next to it. All the leather harnesses were shiny as new and the carriage was gleaming, as was the car.

I said thank you and quickly left. I knew I'd be in trouble if I wasn't back in the house smartish. Gertie later told me that the chauffeur lived in permanent hope that the colonel would go back to using his horse and carriage. John, the chauffeur, had never had a driving lesson but claimed any idiot could drive a car. He wanted to go back to the skills he'd learned with horses 50 years earlier. He hated the change. I never found out if it was true, but I heard that the family was so worried he'd leave when they changed over to the car that they agreed to let him keep the carriage and harness as long as he liked.

That was one of the few instances I came across where a family genuinely seemed to value a servant. The colonel had probably grown up with old John and perhaps that made a difference. I always thought male servants were treated a bit better than us girls anyway. They certainly got paid more for the same sort of work.

But there was something sad about John hoping that the days of horses might come back. When he used to drive the car – and he was apparently a very good driver – he would grumble 'Whoa!' under his breath whenever he applied the brakes, or 'Get on!' when he wanted to go faster. Gertie said he spent his life in his two-room cottage and never had an evening off. He just spent all the time he wasn't driving the family around polishing either the car or the old carriage and its harness.

I was never promoted during my seven years with the colonel and as none of the more senior maids showed any sign of moving on – which would have given me the chance to move up to second housemaid at least – I decided it was probably time for me to go. And if the chauffeur at the colonel's had been an eccentric I was soon to meet some far more bizarre individuals.

Chapter Twenty-Two

I went back to the servants' employment agency and found that the queues were longer than I'd remembered, but that people working there were a little less stiff.

It was 1934 now and, though the worst of the Depression was over, things were still bad, with soup kitchens in the East End and some up West too. Only a very few traders still had horses by now.

My mum was getting on a bit by this time. I went to see her sometimes on my day off if I didn't spend it with Mary. I still gave her some of my earnings, but I'd also bought myself a few trinkets and some nice underwear and other clothing. I thought I was doing very well for myself, but I was warned by Mary not to buy silk underwear unless I was very sure I could keep it hidden. 'You'll get in loads of trouble,' she said. 'You'll get teased by the other girls for being uppity even if they've got silk hidden away too, and if anyone in the family finds out you'll get a warning.' She was right, really. We all knew that silk was for the better classes and not for us. But I took the risk, as I loved it. I also bought myself a bit of jewellery and a new hat. I can remember the excitement of buying that hat. We all loved hats then. Everyone had them. Hats and gloves were so glamorous and yet by the time I was in my 60s no one had the slightest interest in them at all. They'd gone the way of horses. The same goes for fans. Every lady had a fan back then when I started work. So I went to a shop in Bond Street and bought one. I had to take my courage in both hands then because I thought maybe they'll think I'm too common and refuse to sell me one. But they were very nice and didn't look sniffy at all when I bought the cheapest one they had – and it still seemed a fortune to me!

I remember walking down Bayswater Road one Sunday afternoon with my hat and gloves and my fan in my little bag thinking I'm as good as anyone. What a lovely feeling that was.

But back to Massey's. I sat there in the employment agency in my best rig-out and told them I wanted to be a head housemaid somewhere smart. I was no longer the timid girl with the borrowed uniform. I was confident now and spoke up for what I wanted. I even thought I might leave London as several girls had told me via the grapevine that the bigger the family the better the dinner!

In the end the employment agency didn't offer me a job as a head housemaid. They thought that was a bit too much of a promotion. But I got a job as second housemaid in a house near Eaton Square in Belgravia, one of the most fashionable parts of London then. And of course it was still near the park so I could carry on seeing Mary.

The new family I was to work for was distantly related to the royal family and this was their London house.

One or two of the members of this new family were really eccentric, to the point, I think, of being insane. But no one really ever seemed to be bothered about it.

Insanity is very common in the English aristocracy. But from day one I could tell this was a different sort of house. I could tell from the stories that went about the servants' hall.

Neither of my previous two houses had had a servants' hall. Only the really grand houses could boast anything big enough to deserve the name. This Belgravia house really did have a servants' hall, because it was a city copy of the kind of house big landed families had in the countryside.

The servants' hall – actually a big room in the basement – had a long table with enough room for 20 to sit round it at a pinch. The basement kitchen was huge too, bigger than anything I'd ever seen before, and you could tell by the quantity of silver they had that they were very rich.

A footman and the butler used to disappear into the butler's pantry every day to polish and clean it all. And spit on it of course! And there were massive solid silver tureens and wine coolers a couple of feet across. Joseph the butler used to spend hours lovingly working his way over all the silver decoration on them.

I had no choice really but to fit into their system, especially since I was being paid quite a bit more by now. Fitting in meant the usual nonsense about the third housemaid opening all the doors for the second housemaid (that was now me) and for the head housemaid and then all of us trooping through in the right order.

But what amazed me was that a house that was part of a terrace could be so big. The rooms seemed colossal and with fireplaces to match. There were also rooms within rooms and corridors along the back that were barely lit and a wine cellar that seemed to me to stretch miles out under the surrounding roads.

Just to dust the tops of the pillars in some of the rooms needed two men with a ladder. We maids couldn't possibly have done it. There were also massive wooden shutters on the windows of some of the other rooms. I remember you had to give them an almighty tug to get them moving and then they groaned under their own weight as you opened them.

I had quite a nice room in this house. It had a tiny fireplace that one of the lowly maids used to light for me every morning. There was no point in me saying 'Oh don't bother, I'll do it,' or 'Why don't you get a bit more sleep and then come up and do it?'

None of that sort of thing would have been tolerated for a minute. The best I could do was to be as nice as I could and have a little chat with her when she came to do my room. She also made my bed and polished my shoes. With my new socialist hat on I never for a minute said or did anything to make her feel inferior, or at least I hope I didn't. Having someone wait on you a bit like this was your reward for having done the same chores for the upper servants when you were the lowest of the low. The idea was you could look forward to the end of your skivvying days by handing on a bit of skivvying to some other poor soul. I liked Annie, the lowest maid in that Eaton Square house. She was Scottish and always in a good mood and never complained about the work or the hours. Once when she missed her afternoon off because they wouldn't let her go till she'd finished her duties she just shrugged and said, 'Oh it'll save me a bit of money.'

Now I said this house was full of eccentrics and it really was. The first hint of this was when the cook told me I might occasionally have to wait at table. I told her I'd never really done it in a big house but she said, 'Oh the mistress won't mind that.'

I thought that was a bit odd, but didn't think any more about it at the time. Part of being a good servant is that you don't question things – at least not out loud – but I did wonder what she meant. In fact I must have looked a bit surprised because she said, 'Don't worry. There's lots of odd things go on in this house.'

So I saw that even senior servants might judge their masters. If they'd worked for really strict aloof families, servants tended to despise families where things were a bit more lax. On the other hand, though, they might judge their masters for being mad or bad – there was still a tendency to accept that aristocrats had a right to do whatever they liked, even as far as breaking the law.

A few weeks into my new job I was asked to do my first bit of parlour maid work. This was when I found out just what a strange place I'd landed up in.

The day started in the usual way. We housemaids cleaned the fires and brushed the carpets in the various living rooms; then we were having our breakfast in the servants' hall. We were, as usual, sitting in strict order of importance. Cook at the head of the table, with the parlour maids and then housemaids and kitchen maids in order down one side and the footmen and boots – there were half a dozen men – down the other in order of seniority. The kitchen maid and scullery maid sat farthest from the cook with the odd-job boy on the male side opposite.

The ladies' maids never ate with us. In fact, I never saw or met them though I knew there were two. They did everything with and for their mistresses from the moment they woke till the moment they went to bed. Mary used to say, 'They're Siamese twins!'

According to one of the footmen, one of the ladies' maids slept in a bed only ten feet from her mistress because the old lady woke so often in the night and always asked for something. The poor maid never got a full night's sleep.

The butler never sat with us for any meals and nor did the housekeeper. They were as far above us as the family were above them. They ate in the housekeeper's room which was well away from us and were served by the kitchen maid.

It was after our breakfast that I was told to go up along with the parlour maid and serve the family their breakfast. I was very nervous, but the parlour maid, who was called Elsie, told me not to worry. She also said the family insisted on calling her Elsa because Elsie was too common!

Looking back I suspect that explained why other servants I worked with were given new names by their employers.

So up I went, shaking in my boots, and into the breakfast room where the sideboard was laden with kidneys and rice and bacon and all sorts of delicious things. There were just four people at the table: three elderly men and a woman with a green parrot on her shoulder. Now, the thing about the parrot was that it had messed all down her shoulder and all down the front of her dress and she wasn't in the least bothered. She just smiled into the distance and every now and then fed the bird something from her hand.

What amazed me that morning was that the conversation in the dining room didn't miss a beat as we came quietly into the room. The parlour maid put various things on various plates and handed them round the table. I just stood looking awkward. They never spoke to Elsie nor looked at either of us and when, after about five minutes, we left the room, Elsie explained that the elderly woman insisted on having two maids at breakfast even though only one was needed. That was why I'd been left standing there.

At dinner the old lady always had the footmen standing either side of the main double doors into the dining room. We used to call the footmen's clothes half livery because they had a bit of gold braid but they no longer powdered their hair or wore knee breeches. An elderly maid told me that footmen in big houses wore powder in their hair and stockings in some houses until just after the Great War. Footmen were like bits of furniture in some ways or maybe more like diamonds and cut glass in the sense that the more you had the more people were impressed. They were a way to show off your money and status. Quantities of male servants were far more linked to family status than quantities of female servants.

It's hard to believe but footmen were often measured before they were taken on. An interview might consist of the butler measuring round the footman's calf. If he had a big sturdy calf and was six feet tall he'd get the job. If he was skinny and short he'd be shown the door.

But if footmen had to be tall the opposite was true for maids. It was much better if they were short. Employers hated maids to be tall because there was an idea that only the better off were supposed to be tall.

But the world was full of silly ideas in those days – like the one that working-class people's brains were different from those of the better off.

Chapter Twenty-Three

So there I was working for a real crackpot. She had what seemed to me completely batty ideas about everything. The old lady's eccentricity didn't stop at footmen and parrots. In the mornings when we were cleaning the various ground floor rooms – and by the way, no one at that time would have called them reception rooms – I always noticed that there was a lot of food on the dining room carpet.

Dining room carpets were the worst to clean, but here there seemed to be far more food on the floor than you would expect even after a big family meal. I asked the head housemaid about it and she said that the mistress always had two of her favourite dogs sitting at table in the evenings, even if the family had guests. When she was young the mistress had apparently been mad about animals and one of the family legends was that she'd ridden her pony down from Hyde Park and up the front steps and into the hall before leaping off and running upstairs, leaving the pony to one of the footmen.

I gradually got to know the staff in the Belgravia house and realised that they were the usual mix: old servants who were devoted to the family and one or two younger ones who, like me, thought the world was changing and about bloody time too.

I had a sudden increase in my wages after about six months and was told that the family were worried about losing their servants, because the newspapers were starting to talk about how difficult servants were to keep.

This was the beginning of what was often written about as the 'servant problem'. One or two elderly aristocrats in the House of Lords were so worried about being left to make their own tea that they had initiated a debate about making servants sign a contract to stay in a job for several years. They only gave up the idea when they realised that it would mean a family couldn't get rid of someone they didn't like without paying them for the rest of their contract!

Families were still good at getting rid of servants ruthlessly when they felt they had to. It was in this house that I saw a girl asked to leave and shown the door all in the space of one day. Poor Scottish Annie had clearly been seeing a boy. That would have been a route to a right good telling off rather than a sacking if she'd been lucky, but for Annie it was much worse.

A few days before the scandal broke I'd been talking to Annie and I'd noticed she'd put on a bit of weight, which suited her. In fact she looked really well. I had no idea that this might mean much beyond her getting a bit more food and enjoying life. But the day came about a week later when Annie disappeared. No one knew she was about to leave and there was a sort of silence about her that I couldn't understand. When I asked and people looked awkward I thought she'd had a terrible accident and been killed by a bus or something. Of course she *had* had a terrible accident. She'd got pregnant and they rushed her out of the house almost as soon as they found out. It was a rotten thing to do. These so-called Christians who trotted off to church every Sunday showed no charity at all to poor Annie. Anyway they're all dead and gone now and no doubt the good Lord is giving them a severe telling off up there beyond the clouds for all their uncharitable acts.

* * *

I never heard a word about Annie after she left, but I suspect she was as amazed as anyone to find she was pregnant. Girls were so vague about sex, as I say, and we believed all sorts of nonsense about getting rid of unwanted pregnancies. Hot baths we all know about, but we also used to think running would get rid of it or throwing yourself downstairs or drinking masses of hot water with match heads soaked in it. I knew several girls who swore that poking about inside yourself with a knitting needle could do it if you were careful and didn't mind a bit of pain.

What made me really cross about the Annie business was the hypocrisy of it. I realised this about a year later when the mistress of the house wanted things smartened up as her nephew was coming back from America. What was about to happen made me realise that, when it came to sex, there was definitely one rule for the rich and one for the poor.

But by the time it started Annie was only a vague memory. We all knew that she'd been 'ruined' – that was the stupid word everyone used in those days. We knew it was all about sex and shame, and then along came the nephew. He was also apparently an earl's brother and he thought sexual abuse was just a bit of fun.

I didn't even set eyes on him for months after he first arrived, partly because the routines in the house made it very unlikely that the second housemaid would ever bump into the butler let alone a member of the family. But the thing is he must have seen me because hard as I tried, or as we the team of housemaids tried to avoid him, we started to bump into him regularly. If the family wanted to break the rules on how a house was run of course they could, and he would have known that hanging around in the sitting rooms in the afternoon or in the drawing room before breakfast would increase his chances of bumping into us.

The first few times we saw him we just curtseyed and kept our heads down and walked out in line. The head housemaid eventually complained to the housekeeper after this had happened half a dozen times over a period of a few weeks because she knew something was going on. She didn't know what, but I heard her complaining that we couldn't do our work and the old lady would complain if the rooms were dusty – but how could we clean them when he kept popping up?

The head housemaid was old-fashioned and hated criticising the family so it made me smile when I heard her say, 'He can't be right in the head!'

It was all just an inconvenience at first and it didn't bother me because I didn't think for a minute that it might have anything to do with me. We were invisible and I'd never heard of upper-class people having lower-class mistresses or girl-friends. I knew about it much later because long after I left service I read books about how toffs and royalty – especially that dirty old bugger King Edward VII – would walk around pretending to be pillars of respectability, as if they had a moral compass up their bums, while secretly having affairs with showgirls and prostitutes. But in Hoxton we didn't know any upper-class people and girls didn't even dream that some white-gloved toff would come and sweep them away. It just didn't happen.

The people I'd worked for up till then were upper or at least middle class and to them – apart from the groping vicar we were nothing. We were just something they had to have, best hidden away in the basement.

But when I told people what had happened with the earl's brother they said they knew lots of examples of similar behaviour.

I've mentioned that I was a bit of a looker. I'd like to be modest about it but I can't because it was true! The other servants used to kid me and say, 'You want to watch yourself . . . they'll all be after you.' But the uniform made us all look so unattractive that it never occurred to me that someone I worked for might be after me. When the others teased me I thought they meant boys I might meet outside work would be after me. Of course they were, now and then in the park and round the streets, especially on my occasional day back in Hoxton. Every girl knows when she's getting attention!

Chapter Twenty-Four

I got the shock of my life when I set off one Sunday to meet Mary. It was a lovely day as I crossed Park Lane, which was still a lane though busy with cars by now. It was only after the Second World War that it became the bloomin great dual carriageway that it is now.

So I hopped through the gates and set off towards the Round Pond in Kensington Gardens, which was the usual place where I met Mary. I was walking along enjoying myself – it was so lovely to escape that bloody house and all its rules and regulations – when I heard someone walking behind me. Now, every girl knows pretty quickly if the person behind is deliberately walking in such a way that he makes sure he never quite overtakes and I quickly realised that whoever was behind me was doing just that.

I thought whoever it was might be after my bag, though he was an idiot if he was, because he should have known I was not likely to be carrying a sack of gold like the Duchess of Onslow or someone. So I just kept going. Being out of the house brought something of the East End back to me and I thought, 'If he makes a grab at me I'll knock his bleedin' head off.'

I'd got a few hundred yards further when he finally came up alongside me and just started talking. I can't remember exactly what he said. It was just ordinary stuff about the weather but in one of those very upper-class accents that made me embarrassed about opening my mouth at all.

After a bit more blather he said, 'What's your name?' and 'You're awfully pretty. May I walk with you?' It was something along those lines. I still hadn't a clue who he was so I just looked at him, scowled and speeded up a bit. People think we all bowed and scraped to anyone in fine clothes and it's true we did but not quite all the time. If someone was really going to take liberties and there was no chance of getting nicked you might get a faceful of Billingsgate or a smack if you pushed it too far.

When I sped up he dropped back and I just assumed he was a toff out looking for a girl – I mean a prostitute. Fair enough because the park was full of them and they were just trying to make a living.

As it happened I had a nice day with Mary. We mucked about for a while, walked a bit and then had a cup of tea and a cake in the afternoon. At last it was time to get back.

When I reached the house there was a horrible surprise waiting. There, standing outside the servants' door was the man from the park.

He was lounging there like he owned the place which, of course, in a way he did. I didn't realise it till later but he was the earl's brother. The other servants had said the old lady's nephew was back from America, so I put two and two together. I thought 'Oh blimey, here comes trouble,' and I was right. He sort of dodged in front of me and tried to stop me getting back in the house and of course being back at the house meant I had my servile head on! I just blushed and then, I'm ashamed to admit, I started to cry.

He just wouldn't let me pass and he was smiling like he was really enjoying himself. Then, when he'd had his fun, he wandered off towards the front of the house swishing his cane.

There was a bit of relief from my worries about this new pest when, the next day, we were told by the head housemaid that we were all to receive an umbrella from the family as a present. I was really happy to get it a few days later because I thought at least I'll have something to keep the bloomin' rain off and a weapon if I ever need one! And to get a present from your boss was a rare event for a servant. The umbrella was to be one in a series of slightly mad presents I received in this house. Six months after we were told about the umbrella we were told to line up in the servants' hall as the housekeeper, who was in charge of us housemaids, had a surprise for us. She looked furious when we arrived in the hall because I think she thought the family were being silly and as a result making her look silly in front of us.

But she stood there and then said the old lady had insisted we be presented with new cleaning kits. She then walked along and gave each of us a new set of brushes with our initials on the handles. I so wanted to laugh and I could see the others did too, but we kept a straight face and filed out with our ridiculous brushes. The fact that the old lady thought we'd be delighted to receive personalised tools for a servile job we all hated still makes me marvel at how mad that world was. But that was the thing about some upper-class employers. They really thought we enjoyed looking after them and were grateful to them. They'd grown up with the idea that we each had an allotted place and that servants were actually much happier being servants than being rich and pampered as they were. I could imagine the old lady thinking to herself: 'Won't the servants be happy to have their very own equipment!'

She probably also did it because, as I've said, people were really worrying now about losing their servants or at least having to pay them more and more. If we had brushes with our names on we'd never want to leave, would we?

So there we were with our brushes and our umbrellas and the days followed one another all pretty much the same except for the menace of the earl's brother, if that's what he really was. Everyone below stairs called him that but none of us knew if it was really true.

After that incident at the door I tried not to worry. I thought he must have got the message and maybe just fancied teasing someone weaker than he was, someone he knew wouldn't be able to do anything about it without the risk of losing her position. At that stage I didn't realise it was all about sex. That came a few weeks later.

We'd just traipsed back down from our early morning cleaning in the drawing room and the various sitting rooms when the telephone rang in the servants' hall. I took no notice and carried on sorting out my cleaning things. It wasn't unusual for the phone to ring, but we weren't important enough to answer it so we just ignored it. Soon it stopped. Then about ten minutes later the head housemaid disappeared through the door into the servants' hall and came back looking very awkward. She came straight over to me and said, 'The master says you've to stop what you're doing and go up to the drawing room right now.'

I was so dazed I just stupidly said, 'What, now?'

'Yes, now,' said the head housemaid. So off I went up the servants' stairs and through the door at the back of the hall across to the drawing room door. I knocked and waited and didn't hear a sound. I was really nervous by now because if the old lady or anyone saw me there on my own outside hours – I mean at a time when I wasn't cleaning – I'd get a terrific telling off and maybe even the sack.

But another bit of me thought it wouldn't matter anyway because the only reason I could have been called upstairs at this hour was to be told to pack my stuff and get out. I remembered that embarrassing business with the earl's brother and I assumed he'd complained about me. Even if he'd made up a pack of lies or said I'd assaulted him there would be no point in putting my side of the story. It was going to be that old problem: who'd believe a girl from Hackney against the word of the brother of an earl? It's strange when you think something like that is going to happen and there's nothing you can do about it – no workers' rights back then! You quickly get resigned to the idea.

So I was thinking to myself as I stood there, 'It's back to Massey's for you my girl and with no reference.' Then the door opened a bit and there he was – the bloody earl's brother, large as life and twice as ugly. My stomach turned over at the sight of him. He just looked down his nose at me, grinned a bit and said, 'Come in.' He was staring at me and I stood there like a naughty kid not knowing which way to look or what to do with myself.

Apart from the fact that I was a bit scared I half wanted to kill him for putting me through all this. He asked if I wanted to sit down and I said no. It was such a stupid question. He must have known that no servant was ever allowed to sit in the presence of a member of the family. I just kept looking at the floor and mumbling. I felt such a fool. I was completely intimidated.

Then he said: 'Do you need any money? I'm quite happy to pay you, you know.'

I just said, 'No, thank you Sir,' thinking he's definitely got a screw loose, this one. I still hadn't really twigged that this was all about sex. He wanted to have sex with me. That's what 'I'm happy to pay you,' had meant. Then he came over to me, very close, and said, 'That will be all for now. You may go.' I was so flustered that I turned my back on him to walk out. As I went towards the door he walked behind me and patted my bottom a couple of times. After the groping vicar in my first job and now this, I was beginning to think it was all my fault.

Mind you I knew enough about the world by now not to be upset. I just thought he must be mad. I was also angry in a sort of hopeless way. I went downstairs and didn't say a word to the other servants, particularly the other housemaids who gave me some very odd looks. I was friendly with them but didn't think I could tell them what had just happened, but I thought I'd definitely talk to Mary about it.

I had to wait a few days till Sunday, my day off, but I went to bed that night feeling confused about what to do. Should I give in my notice and set off for Massey's straight away or wait a bit and see what happened?

When my duties were finally finished at about ten o'clock I

went to bed and lay there is the dark, thinking. Then the other housemaid suddenly said: 'Is he after you?'

I didn't say anything but she went on, 'He's got a terrible reputation. I think he was in trouble with the police. There were loads of rumours about him. He stayed here for six months a few years ago, but they always pack him off in the end. He's just trouble that one, for all his airs and graces and nice voice. I'd steer clear of him if I were you.'

I lay there thinking she was probably right, but when I met Mary that Sunday I was amazed at what she said.

We'd agreed to go to Southend on our day off. As this was going to be the first time I'd ever left London I was really excited about it – at least until the business with the earl's brother started. That had put a bit of a damper on our outing. But I didn't want to spoil it for Mary so we met as usual at half past ten. As we weren't going to be gadding about Kensington High Street and Notting Hill as we usually did, we met at Victoria station, which was just a ten-minute walk for me.

I saw her waiting. She was in her best rig-out and I was so pleased to see her that I forgot all about my little problem. We wanted to save a bit of money so we walked all the way to Liverpool Street station. It took about an hour, maybe more, but we didn't mind as we always talked our heads off. After a bit I told her about what was happening at work and she stopped, threw her head back and laughed.

'He just wants to get in yer knickers,' she said.

'It's nothing to laugh about,' I said. I was almost cross but it was hard to be cross with Mary.

'I should be so lucky,' she said. 'I'd go with a chimney sweep if he'd have me – they're lucky and all. He's just havin' a laugh,' she said. 'You're too pretty for your own good. Don't take it so seriously. Tell you what – just give him the run around. Tell him you'll meet him one afternoon or something and then just don't turn up. And tell him you need ten bob before you can do it. When he gets hold of you next time after that, make an excuse about why you didn't turn up and make another arrangement and then don't turn up again. Tell him you need a bit more money too. If he gets really mad at you and tries any funny business tell 'im you've got the clap or that you're going to wet yourself!'

At this she had to stop walking again she was laughing so much.

I thought about what she said as we walked along and realised she was right in a way. After all, I was no wilting violet. I could look after myself.

So far he'd been able to intimidate me because he was more or less my employer and at work you had to have your subservient head on. But if he was going to break the rules then so was I.

I told Mary I'd take her advice and see what happened. 'If the worst comes to the worst,' she said, 'you can just leave.'

Once again she was right. There was always loads of work out there and the money was on the up. The poor old things we worked for couldn't do a thing without us. They'd never learned. And now they were getting in a panic.

Chapter Twenty-Five

By the time we'd got to Liverpool Street and found a couple of seats on the train I'd forgotten all about it. I was so excited by all the noise, the steam and the smoke. When we set off I was amazed how all the blackened houses and factories suddenly ended and there were green fields everywhere as far as I could see. There were a few cars but no big roads and still lots of horses working on the land. It was so pretty to me, used to London grime. Essex was still really green back then – countryside bloody everywhere, as we used to say.

A lot of Londoners felt lost outside their own areas but I loved getting away that day and Mary and I agreed we'd do it again as soon as we could. Mary had brought along four hard-boiled eggs for us as a treat for breakfast. How on earth she'd managed to boil them in the house where she worked I'll never know. It just wasn't allowed, but she was a right risk-taker was Mary and not really afraid of anyone.

When we got to Southend we walked around looking in the shop windows at the clothes. Mary was mad about hats – even worse than me.

And she didn't mind a bit going in a shop and pretending to be wealthy and talking down to the staff, which is what wealthy people did. I went in with her a few times but I could hardly keep from laughing because you could see that the shop people suspected something was up but they weren't quite sure. She'd la-di-dah them in a loud confident voice and try on a few very expensive hats and then we'd bolt out of the shop and run down the road screeching.

We got caught out a bit on this day in Southend because after messing about in a hat shop and then running away we had chips on the end of the pier. There we saw the shopkeeper walking past us giving Mary a very dirty look.

Mary didn't give a damn. She stared straight back and stuck out her tongue.

I didn't believe Mary when she said we could get a train along the pier and go out to sea on it. But she was right and it was a marvel. The little train was packed when we got on it but it was like the Eiffel Tower and the Empire State Building all rolled into one for someone like me who'd never seen anything. The train was fun too because there was a man singing in our carriage. He sang a few music hall songs which was lovely for us. This was the first time I'd ever seen the sea, which seemed enormous and a bit sad I thought because there was almost nothing there. Just emptiness and only an occasional tiny ship like a dot in the distance.

Mary was a strange girl. You'd think she'd hardly know anything, yet here she was always coming out with amazing stuff. She once told me that humans were just apes with big heads. I remember laughing and thinking she was having me on. But she was right – and I only found out about 30 years later! I wondered how the hell she knew it all with her background. She once told me that before she met me she spent a lot of her free time in libraries on her own, so that might have been it, but then she was a very slow reader. She was brave and quick in her own way and she loved finding things out. I miss her every day although she's long dead.

So we got back to Southend station at about six that evening, bursting with ice cream and fish and chips, and exhausted. We were so tired we fell into a deep sleep on the train. I woke up with a start some time later, shook Mary and said, 'Quick! We mustn't miss our stop.'

'Don't be a clot,' she said and gave me a push. 'How can we miss our stop when the train doesn't go any further than London?'

And with that she went straight back to sleep but this time with her head in my lap. We had tea in a Lyons tea shop half way across London on the walk back and, do you know, that was one of the few places where servants didn't get looked down on. The nippies were what really made the Lyons tea shops. That's what we called the Lyons waitresses. They were always very sweet and polite. No wonder Lyons lasted so long – into the 1960s I believe.

I felt like I was getting somewhere that evening. Sitting by the window sipping my tea and eating lovely iced buns, I felt I'd come such a long way from Hoxton. I had some money. My mum had told me to keep most of it – she only wanted a few shillings a month now – but I usually sent her more. In that tea shop with Mary I felt like I might really get somewhere in life and, if not that, then I might at least escape in the end from the drudgery of domestic work. As I sat there I realised I didn't want to go back to my gloomy room at the top of that old house. I wanted more of a life of my own and not to be reminded every day that I wasn't as good as other people.

You hardly knew it in the 1930s because you were only a tiny cog in the big machine, but things were changing even more rapidly then, which is probably why I had that confident feeling in the tea shop. All the horses had gone pretty much and a lot of the East End seemed somehow cleaner and tidier to me, less poor, when I went back now and then.

I decided I wasn't going to be ground down like the older servants. As the 1930s wore on the working classes were getting more confident and everyone knew it at some level. I was just as good as the people I worked for. After all, I knew how to clean and tidy and work hard and they didn't know anything except getting up late and eating and pestering girls!

So the spirit of rebellion got into me and I persuaded Mary to stay out later than ten that night we came back from the seaside. I crept in at about ten thirty and went straight to bed and thought nothing more about it. No one seemed to be around. But next morning I got summoned after another one of those scary phone calls to the servants' hall.

'You've to see the old lady,' I was told. 'Right now.' More and more we were calling her the old lady now instead of the mistress. I think even one or two older servants were starting to get a bit fed up. They probably knew people outside who worked in factories and that that gave you freedom in your spare time. Anyway, up the back stairs I went but not with my tail between my legs. 'If she behaves like a cow I'm off,' I said to myself, 'and I'll write my own bloody reference.' I knew several girls who'd either written their own or got someone they knew to write them a reference. I'd have done anything now my blood was up.

I knocked on the drawing room door as timid as you like, thinking, 'She's going to give me a terrible telling off.' I tried not to look surly but I expect I did – well, servile with a hint of stroppy, as Mary used to say.

She was about three sentences into her little speech and I'd hardly begun to take it in when I realised to my amazement that she wasn't telling me off at all. I think that was the day I got the biggest surprise of my whole life – never before or since have I been so shocked.

I can remember exactly what she said and how she said it.

She said: 'I want to apologise for the fact that you have been very shabbily treated by a member of my family. I'm so sorry if you have been upset by it. It's disgraceful and if there is anything I can do you must let me know. Would you like to sit down?'

I just stood there like an idiot, because this was the last thing I expected. But there she was apologising to me and asking if I wanted to sit down. It was enough to make you religious! I just said, 'Thank you Ma'am,' and stood staring dumbly into space.

I was cross with myself afterwards because of course my reaction would have confirmed the old view that all servants are stupid even when you are nice to them. I would have liked to thank her properly but I was just too surprised.

After a pause she said: 'Well, that's all and I want to assure you the problem will not arise again.' I curtseyed and out I went – backwards of course.

That incident changed my attitude to things generally. I realised that employers could be human and, looking back, I realise that this was a further sign that times were changing. I think the old lady did have some genuine feeling for me. I've no idea how she found out I'd been pestered, but she clearly knew everything and that was typical of big houses then. It was very hard to keep secrets.

She was true to her word and I was never pestered by her relative again. In fact he was sent packing, I should imagine, as I never laid eyes on him again. Fifty years earlier I'd have probably been sacked for encouraging him.

I couldn't help feeling grateful to the old lady for her apology and it did make me feel that this was one house where at least I would be safe. I no longer felt I had to leave as soon as possible. I could take my time until I had a better job to go to or a nice handsome husband.

I was getting quite well paid by now – nearly £33 a year, which was good for a housemaid, and I felt I'd had a sort of victory. And as I said to Mary, the old lady must have meant what she said when she apologised because she wasn't wearing her parrot!

After this the weeks flew by more happily than ever before. I saw Mary regularly and we sometimes got chatting to soldiers over by Knightsbridge barracks. I was delighted one Sunday when a young soldier – he was very handsome if a bit short and spotty – said to me, 'You don't need to give me sixpence for walking round the park with you. I should be paying you, you're so pretty!'

Well, I was delighted by that. Blushing and giggling like a 15-year-old, I was. When we parted he didn't make a grab at me – like so many of them. Mind you, in his case, I wouldn't have minded as he was so good looking. I don't think that particular one would have minded me being a servant either, but I didn't fancy a soldier's wife's life. I knew I'd worry he'd be injured and I might not see him for months or even years at a time.

Chapter Twenty-Six

I don't want it to sound as if it was all misery and hard work in that house. There were some really fun moments when the strict servant hierarchy eased off a bit.

About once every couple of months, for example, we had what we called a ratting evening. Some of the servants who'd started life in the country used to organise it and it had been done for years by the time I worked there.

The rattings were organised to catch the mice – and sometimes rats – that plagued the kitchens. Of course as I've explained the kitchens in these big old houses were usually kept spotless and the pots and pans, plates and various utensils were all cleaned and put away every day; but these were old houses with damp cellars and rotten wet brickwork and hollows in the walls everywhere. We used to say that the real owners of the house were the vermin because there were always far more of them.

You could get poison for mice but we weren't allowed to use it – it was very dangerous to leave lying about. As a result there were mice everywhere. You'd often see one dart across the downstairs hall or the servants' hall or through the kitchen. We didn't take much notice, but they sometimes got in the pantry and though we didn't mind the family eating mouse poo, we didn't want to eat it ourselves. The solution was the ratting evening.

One of the men would collect the gardener's terrier late in

the evening and bring it into the house. The kitchen would have been left empty for an hour or so which usually encouraged a few mice to show themselves. One dim light would be left on and then we'd crowd round and slowly open the door. When it was open wide enough we'd push the terrier through and he knew just what to do. He'd scuttle about like a mad thing trying to catch any mice that were rushing about on the floor. If any mice on the shelves or cupboards froze, one of the footmen or the kitchen maid would run through with a duster, trying to knock them on to the floor where the terrier could get at them. That terrier could catch half a dozen in as many seconds. We'd try the pantry too and the servants' hall in the same way. Some evenings we'd catch a dozen or more mice. The half-dozen servants who always gathered to watch loved it. I must admit it was always a flurry of excitement on a dull, cold winter's night.

I wondered why they didn't just get a cat until someone told me that the old lady didn't like cats. It always seemed odd that she preferred a mice-infested kitchen. Catching a few mice every now and then with the terrier was never going to get rid of them.

For all the work we did the house was disgustingly unhygienic in many ways, at least compared to modern houses. With no fridge, a mean-minded mistress could insist that meat that was rotten was still used. Cook would be told to give it a good boil before roasting it to make sure the germs were killed. Often she would be told to feed the old meat to the servants. And if a piece of meat was left that long, there was a good chance that the mice might have been at it.

There was an idea that if food was well cooked it didn't matter if it had been dropped on the floor a few times or had mould on it. As long as it looked all right once it arrived at the table I don't think they cared, and of course they couldn't check everything we did. They had to take it on trust even though they were trusting people who often didn't like them and felt they were treated badly. We were bound to end up spitting in their soup now and then!

It was the same with the flour, which often had weevils in it, and under the skirting boards there were huge numbers of silverfish. We just accepted insects – like the bedbugs that most people had to put up with – because you couldn't get rid of them.

So we had our fun with the rattings and then there was dancing and clubs. Mary and I heard about a social club for servants – it turned out there were quite a few of these – so we went along to see if there might be dancing. Well, there was a bit – but it was very prim and proper and we were lectured a bit about our moral welfare. This annoyed me so much we gave it up. We wanted the sort of smooching that wasn't allowed.

A lot of people then, particularly older people, still thought that the waltz was immoral because you stood too close to your partner. I remember seeing a poster that said: 'Don't threaten your immortal soul. Reject the immoral waltz!'

But then we discovered the Hammersmith Palais. How we loved it. It wasn't too far from where I worked so I'd meet up with Mary on our nights off and we'd almost run down Kensington High Street and past Olympia to get to Shepherd's Bush and then Brook Green and that marvellous hall. There was an ice rink there, too, at this time. The first time I tried skating I thought, this is bloody impossible. We still had fairly long skirts then – it would have been about 1937 – and we couldn't afford lessons so we clung to each other and stumbled around for an hour and then got on with the real business of dancing.

Jazz bands were the big thing at the Palais back then. Although I loved waltzing and the foxtrot and other old dances we loved trying the new ones, partly because older people really hated them but also because they left you so breathless with excitement. I remember practising the Charleston in my room back at the house and being told off for making such a racket with my heels on the floor. So after that Mary and I used to practise in the park. We'd hang on to each other and kick our heels outwards and upwards till we could hardly stand for laughing.

We used to dance together at the Palais, too, and no one then thought it meant we were lesbians. Lots of girls danced together. It was just a laugh. Mary and I used to stand at the side of the dance floor and look around at all the plush velvet and the lights. Then there was the cinema we used to go to. The Electric in Portobello Road was a cramped little place and we preferred the big Picture Palace. Mary and I used to cry when almost anything happened in a film, but Mary was a devil and if someone did something nasty on the screen she'd sometimes shout out, 'Oi, leave her alone you pig! Pick on someone your own size.' We'd then have a fit of the giggles. Once it got so bad we were asked to leave.

Mary was always up for a laugh at the dance hall, too. I remember once she came back after being asked to dance by a nice Irishman we saw there every now and then.

'That bloke's made me black and blue,' she said. 'Thinks I'm a bloody sheep he's throwing in the back of a cart!'

She was always coming out with phrases like that.

The Palais was full of Irish fellers back then and my memory is they were all very polite, but half the time we couldn't understand a word they were saying. You didn't hear foreign accents much in London then.

We saw a black man – I mean a really black man – once in Hoxton when I was home for a Sunday and my mouth dropped open. He was smiling at everything and wandering along the road talking to himself. I think he was a bit touched because a friend told me she saw him often and he was always the same: smiling and talking to himself. Black people were so rare then there was no race prejudice. They were like a novelty – part of the street entertainment. Everyone paused to glance after him but no one was rude to him or shouted. I thought he was a handsome devil. Lovely teeth and polished skin like a nice bit of furniture!

Chapter Twenty-Seven

I had my first proper kiss at the Palais – I'd been kissed a few times in the park on my evenings off by boys that Mary and I got talking to but it was always a bit rushed.

They were also usually too rough or just gave you a hard peck on the cheek or straight away tried to stick their tongues right in your mouth. I thought that was disgusting. Stick your tongue back at them said Mary and she swore that's what she used to do – they run a mile when you do that, she said.

For a long time I just couldn't understand why there was such a fuss about this kissing lark. It looked nice in the films when there was lots of music and they said nice things to each other with their eyes half closed and all dreamy-like. But I still used to think, 'Why are they taking so bloomin' long about it and pretending they're going to faint?' Mary was always hilarious about kissing. When it was a passionate kiss in the cinema she'd lean over to me and say, 'Fuckin 'ell, he's hungry – he's havin 'er for his dinner.' She had a terrible mouth on her sometimes.

So there I was at the Palais when this very nice boy came up to me and asked me to dance. He was lovely – dark hair, tall and with a lovely smile. So many people had terrible teeth back then that you really noticed when someone had good gnashers. I didn't even glance at Mary as he spoke to me. We had a rule that we never looked each other in the eye when a boy asked one of us to dance in case we got the giggles. We had terrible bouts of the giggles a few times and the result was usually that the boy went off horribly embarrassed. So I smiled at this boy and we whooshed around the floor for a bit and I thought, what a lovely dancer.

I wasn't up to much on the floor but I could just about avoid breaking my partner's toes. This time, and it was the first time I felt it, I knew why the films made a fuss about all this dancing and swooning. It felt lovely – better than any other dance I'd had. I was really sad when it was over. He dropped me back where Mary was standing at the edge of the dancers when the music stopped but instead of going away he stayed to talk. He talked to Mary as well and wasn't a bit shy, which was unusual. So we had a lovely time and then he said he'd walk us to the bus stop. We told him we'd have to go by nine to get back in time. We didn't tell him where we were off to out of habit. One hint that we were domestics and he might be off like a shot.

So he followed us out and Mary dropped back a bit which was lovely of her. She was sensitive like that sometimes – if she wasn't in the mood to tease you to bits. When we got to the bottom of Kensington Church Street just by the gardens he said he had to go. We'd been talking for nearly half an hour and he'd made Mary catch up and join in – which made me a little cross I must admit. Then right in front of Mary he leant over and gave me a long slow kiss right on the mouth.

People say your heart stops or time stops or something and when it's never happened you think, 'Oh yes, pull the other one,' but I can remember that kiss all those years ago as if it was everything happy you could ever have rolled up into a few seconds. And it was all dreamy just like in the films!

That boy asked me if we were going to be at the Palais the following Wednesday so we said yes and off he wandered. I was so excited I could hardly get through the week.

'Oh gawd, she's smitten,' said Mary, I obviously looked a bit upset at being teased so she said, 'Blimey, you really are. Sorry.'

And she was really sweet after that as we walked back round the park. She left me half way home and I got in after ten – late again but I got away with it. I think the other staff had heard what happened with the earl's brother and had been told to be nice to me for a while.

I hardly slept that night even though I knew I'd be exhausted as a result at the end of the next day. The week took forever to get through and I kept being scolded by the head housemaid for not concentrating or for dropping things. I was in love, that's the truth, and when Wednesday came around again I was off across the park like a greyhound to meet Mary. I'd also spent ages making myself look nice with a bit of makeup and a lot of scrubbing.

We got to the Palais in record time and would you believe it? He never turned up. That was my first big disappointment in the love department. In some ways I never got over it because he didn't hang around long enough for me to find out about all his bad habits. Even now I find it hard to believe he had any but I suppose he must have done. Mary, as usual, came to the rescue and cheered me up. But I was in no mood for dancing with anyone else so we didn't bother to stay long. We went for a walk down by the river at Hammersmith and though Mary wanted me to talk about my disappointment the whole experience had made me feel so bad that I insisted we change the subject.

We talked about London and the river. I was such an ignorant girl that I couldn't understand how the river at Hammersmith could be the same as the river in the East End. Mary laughed at this but in a nice way. She tried to make me forget my troubles by pretending to speak cockney which she did really well. I remember I couldn't help smiling when she said, 'Give us a butchers at yer crust' – which meant she wanted to have a look (butcher's hook) at my head (crust of bread). That girl should have been on stage.

Once she made her mind up to find out about something she really picked it up quickly, so as we walked along the river she kept coming out with really funny bits of slang – she told me I was marbles (that's marbles and conkers which means bonkers or mad) and that we needed a tiddly (tiddly wink – drink).

I was a cockney and I didn't know half the words she knew, and she was supposed to be a country girl.

I felt better by the time she dragged me into a smoky little pub miles from anywhere. 'Sod 'em if they think we're tarts,' she said, as she pushed the door open. In those days girls on their own were just starting to be acceptable in a lot of pubs because until the 1930s most men thought girls on their own in a pub were prostitutes. Anyway, one glare from Mary at the barman told him we meant business, so we had a couple of drinks and then set off for the long walk back.

By the time all this happened I'd been in service for nearly ten years. The only holiday I'd had was between my jobs – you weren't allowed a week off, let alone a fortnight, back then. I remember asking Mrs Williams in the house I'd started work in, the one behind Oxford Street, if I could have time off. She'd said, 'What on earth do you mean, time off? You mean you expect me to pay you when you are not working? Don't be absurd.' It was that 'don't be absurd' I really remember as if it was ridiculous that a servant should have an interest that didn't involve her employer.

Now and then Mary and I used to meet other servants from different houses in the area at the Round Pond in Kensington Gardens on Sunday mornings if we had nothing better to do. And you could tell from what they talked about that they weren't prepared to put up with this any more. And already some servants were getting a bit of paid holiday – or at least that's what we heard.

It was around this time that one of the girls I knew a little said, 'Have you heard, there's a union for us lot?' I hadn't heard a word but she explained that if we paid a bit we'd have someone to fight our battles for us. I thought it was a great idea because I knew a bit about unions and thought they'd get our wages up and stop our employers treating us like dirt.

But the domestics' union never really took off because we skivvies were all over the country. And we could hardly ever meet and get organised because we worked such long hours. If you were a maid in a remote Welsh valley how could you ever get to a meeting?

I heard of girls who were told they'd be sacked if they had anything to do with the union and that put a lot of people off. It made me furious but what could we do? It was domestic service, a factory or the workhouse for us. Getting the dole was very difficult; it was just a pittance and there was a lot of shame attached to taking it.

But I never really knew why I didn't jack it all in and go for a job at a factory. I think I was worried it might be worse or dirtier than domestic service. And of course once I'd met Mary I didn't want to move away to some factory in the East End where most of the factories were and not be able to see her. And like me, Mary didn't like the idea of a factory even if it did pay a bit more. We used to try to persuade each other and we had dreams about getting a little place to live together but it all came to nothing. It just seemed impossible. In those days you needed references for everything and there was so much prejudice against servant girls. We thought we'd be laughed at if we tried to rent somewhere together that wasn't just a slum room. And we probably would have been.

Apart from seeing Mary on days and afternoons off my main memory of that time is boredom and repetition. You had to be like a machine to get by. Do your work every day, don't complain, curtsey and just carry on; so that's what we did.

Even Christmas wasn't much of an affair. We got the day off but had to be back on Boxing Day. Anyone who lived miles away couldn't see their family. On Christmas morning the old lady came down with her eldest son and other members of the family, and we traipsed up to her and were given a gift. All the housemaids and kitchen maids were given soap, but the lower down the scale you were the less you got and the cheaper it was!

There were shops that sold gifts – including soap – that were advertised as suitable for servants. When I was drying the soap in the bedrooms I could see the difference. It was a lovely sort of rich-smelling stuff while the soap we got at Christmas was more like carbolic.

To be fair to the family they just did what they'd always done. The habit of treating servants in a certain way went very deep. They'd inherited it from their parents and grandparents and change came very slowly.

Now all that has gone it's very hard to believe how it was, but on those Christmas mornings you have to imagine us all lined up – kitchen maid, house boy, scullery maid, three housemaids and parlour maid. And then we would go up to the family who stood awkwardly in a line. Then you'd take your gift, curtsey and walk back to the line before the next person down the ranking would go up and do the same thing. Then with pained smiles the family would disappear back up the stairs, not to be seen in the basement for another year. The butler and housekeeper and cook were given their presents in a different way and in a different place and we never saw it.

Chapter Twenty-Eight

I went less often to Hoxton, but still kept in touch. They wanted to know all about the house and the dances I went to on my evenings off. In fact, working up West I was a bit of a celebrity with a bit of money and a few nice clothes. I was cock of the bleedin' walk as we used to say.

The months and then years went by. You'd be surprised how hard it was to get close to the people you worked with day in day out. Mary was my best friend and though I liked the house-maids I worked with – even the head housemaid – there was always a slight sense that because you were above some servants and below others real friendships were hard to develop.

But I always had Mary, who was like my magic friend. Looking back, I wish I'd been nicer to many people I worked with – especially the kitchen maid I gave my chocolate to. I always smiled at her or winked or gave her a hug if no one else was about but somehow it never went beyond that. Other girls would sometimes try to be friendly to me – one parlour maid I remember used to catch me for a chat now and then – but I was awkward about it knowing the servants' code about mixing.

I was nearly 26 when I met that boy at the Palais who then disappeared. After him I became much more aware of men looking at me. Girls can always tell when a man looks in a certain way. I can't say how but they always know and I wasn't short of admirers. In fact I sometimes had admirers I could do without.

Some girls slept with the people they worked for – we heard stories now and then. Usually it was the sons and they'd pay the girl a bit of money or take her out and try to meet her after work without the rest of the family knowing. But they always got found out in the end and it was the girl who suffered. She might be mug enough to think a posh boy might marry her, but it never happened, or at least I never heard of it happening. The boy might even tell her he'd marry her, but it was perfectly acceptable for a gentleman to lie to a servant girl or someone in the lower orders. Lying to a servant didn't really count in their eyes as a lie at all. The girl would usually be kicked out at a moment's notice and not a word said to the son who would just carry on with his life as if nothing had happened and it was all just a bit of a laugh.

I was too smart for any of that but I knew that my best way out of domestic service was to get married.

I think I was so sad after the Palais boy disappeared that I was a little vulnerable for a while. So I didn't really pay any attention when one of the footmen, who I'd hardly noticed, started to pay a bit more attention to me and to mysteriously pop up on the back stairs when I was going to and from my work. Then one day he said, 'Hello. Why don't we meet on your day off?'

I thought: here we go again. In those days it didn't take long to get very wary of boys. That old saying about them only being after one thing was definitely true. The girls wanted marriage and the boys wanted sex. It was a trade off. We gave them the sex only after we'd got them to marry us. Terrible, really.

I thought one of the best things that happened in my lifetime was the invention of the pill. Why shouldn't a girl have sex when she likes, just like a boy does? That's what I thought. That swoony evening when I'd kissed that boy from the Palais was lovely because it made me want to have sex – that was what the warm feeling was all about. I don't mind saying it, but I knew I might get pregnant and then he'd most likely be off like a shot and I'd be out on the street. So the thing I wanted I couldn't have.

Even in the East End where girls had tough husbands and boyfriends and had babies really early it was the same. You just got married because that's what you did. I wish the 1960s hadn't been too late for me. I'd have had a wild old time I can tell you!

Anyway, when the footman, who was a nice lad, asked me to meet him on his day off I told him no thanks, but not in an angry way. I smiled and tripped off down the stairs without another word. When I glanced back he looked sad and disappointed. I noticed that. But he was persistent and when I bumped into him again he said, 'I don't want to upset you, so if you don't want to meet me after work I won't ask you ever again.'

I thought that was very polite and actually male domestic servants did tend to be much nicer than factory boys or even soldiers. I hate to admit it but they did learn manners in a grand house, mostly just watching the people they worked for. It might have been skin deep in some cases but not all.

So when he asked me the second time I said, 'I'm off on Wednesday evening and we could walk along a bit, but I can't see you on my Sunday off.' Sunday was reserved for Mary. He just nodded and then when next Wednesday came around he appeared out of nowhere as I went down the street. He made me jump and without thinking I said, 'You're like a bloody ghost. Where did you pop up from?'

We chatted as we walked along, but I told him I couldn't see him for long as I was meeting my friend. Then I told him I'd meet him the next week, again on my half-day off, if he liked. Wasn't I a forward girl!

When I told Mary I was going to see him the next week she made a face like she'd sucked on a lemon.

'Dropping me for a bloody footman,' she said, but she was half joking. 'I'll come along and make sure he doesn't grab yer tits,' she said. 'A delicate upper-class bird like you needs to be looked after among roughs.'

That sort of larking was what she always did. I told her I didn't think it would get much beyond a walk in the park, but that he was a nice boy and that if I didn't get any practice at going out with boys I'd never find a husband. She just smiled at that.

Mary never talked about getting a husband herself. I only thought about it years later, which shows how selfish I was. But at the time she was so good at getting me to talk and hardly said anything about herself unless I really pushed her. Even then she looked uncomfortable so I didn't try too hard. So we said no more about it and I didn't see my footman again – he was called Henry Smith – until I hopped out of the house about four o'clock the following Wednesday afternoon.

I was just thinking to myself as I went along: 'I bet he doesn't bloody turn up now and I'll miss my evening with Mary.'

Then like a bloomin' ghost again he popped up next to me looking almost unrecognisable in his smart suit. Men always wore suits then – no sign of jeans anywhere! He'd made a big effort and had slicked his hair back and looked quite handsome, I thought.

But truth to tell I was still thinking about the boy from the dance hall – poor Henry wasn't as handsome or charming. But we went along and he suggested we have tea at a Lyons, so that's what we did. When I think back I realise that, when I wasn't working, I spent my life in the park and in tea shops!

We had a lovely time in the tea shop, but he was quite a serious character so it wasn't as much of a laugh as it would have been with Mary. She'd have chatted up the waitresses or done impersonations of people at other tables. It was like living dangerously – you never knew when she'd get you into trouble.

If Henry wasn't as much fun, it was probably because he was

nervous, but he did tell me a few funny stories. He said that the family insisted on calling him Harry even though his name was Henry. He hadn't a clue why and he wasn't a militant like me so it didn't bother him much. 'They probably think Henry sounds too grand for a footman,' he said. He also said that when the old lady had guests – which she did every couple of months – he had to stay up all night in one or other of the three corridors off which the bedrooms were situated. After a while he got to know which guests the old lady wanted him to keep an eye on. There was one relative of hers from up north, he said, who had stayed a few times. Whenever this young man stayed Henry was told to position himself as close as possible to the young man's bedroom door and to sit there, on a hall chair, all night. He told me that the first time he had to do this night duty he hadn't really been told why, but as he sat nodding off on the hard chair at about three in the morning he heard a door opening and saw the young man peeping out. He caught the young man's eye and looked down again quickly in true servant fashion. The bedroom door then clicked shut again and he realised the young man had gone back inside. Henry reckoned the old lady just wanted to make sure her friskier guests didn't go wandering and trying to get into the ladies' – or more often the maids' – bedrooms!

Henry told me that when he'd stayed in the old lady's country house, guests were always sneaking around at night and into each other's bedrooms. He said: 'They don't mind if other men sleep with their wives because they are at it themselves, and no one cares so long as no one ever mentions what's going on. I knew two men who seemed to be the best of friends over breakfast and played billiards and all sorts but they definitely shared their wives. It's just what toffs do.'

I wasn't at all shocked when he told me this over tea and cakes. I was used to tales such as this by now and nothing the upper classes got up to would have surprised me. But it was something else to tell Mary next time we met. I knew she'd love it.

I liked Henry but he didn't quite do it for me, if you know

what I mean. There wasn't that spark and more than anything it was the spark I wanted. He was one of those men who told lots of stories and it was sheer luck whether it was worth listening to or not. He was hit and miss. If you fell asleep half way through a story it would never put him off. He'd just keep going in a harmless but sweet sort of way. It was like he was oblivious to everyone. I think he'd learned as a boy to turn his brain off because, as he used to say himself, he'd been in service since he was a foetus. I had to ask him what a foetus was!

He told me one really good story. He was working at a big house in Hertfordshire. The family had a son about his age – Henry was just a boy at the time. This boy insisted on taking him fishing down at one of the estate ponds. Whatever they caught they put, still alive, in a big bucket. Then Henry had to carry the bucket. It was heavy as it had about a gallon of water in it to keep the fish alive. Walking behind the young man, he would carry the bucket up to the house where all the fish, still alive and kicking, were tipped into a big tin bath which Henry then had to fill up with water. All the family would then traipse down to admire the fish.

When they'd finished, the young man would say, 'Henry, put them back in the pond would you?'

Poor Henry had to lug the bucket of fish back down to the lake. He had to do this once, sometimes twice a week and no account was taken of these extra duties by the butler. Henry still had to do all his other duties, which included boot cleaning, waiting on the other servants and so on.

A week after we'd been out on a second date the head housemaid told me the housekeeper had told her to tell me not to be seen outside the house with Henry again or we'd both be in trouble. So that was the end of that. They tried to control every minute of your life, but this time I didn't really mind.

But one really good thing came of Henry. On our second date he had introduced me to a friend of his, a young man named John.

When I stopped going out with Henry I went back to my regular trips with Mary. But I noticed that she'd changed a bit. In fact I'd noticed it gradually over the previous six months or even a year. Somehow she had lost a bit of her sense of fun. I began to think life was getting her down a bit.

'I'll never get out of this bloody hole,' she used to say now and then. She still larked about like she did in the old days but it wasn't quite the same.

She still came up with outrageous stories about the house where she worked but she never told me anything that was ordinary. She always looked glum and changed the subject when I asked her about herself and her plans.

But she still loved exaggerating to make me laugh and it was around this time that she told me one of her best stories. It was about 'her' family going to their house in Scotland.

When they went up each summer half the servants went with them and half stayed at home in London. She told me that once they'd gone the remaining servants, the footmen and housemaids, used to try to get the housekeeper drunk so they could have wild parties at night.

She told outrageous lies about servants. 'The first footman had the biggest mickey I've ever seen in my life,' she used to say and then she'd hold her hands about a foot apart. 'And do you know, as you go down the footmen in rank their mickeys get smaller. It's a known fact throughout the world of domestic service. All footmen are the same. As they get promoted they get bigger and by the time they're made butler they have to get a licence for it, it's so big.'

She also had some funny stories about women that she loved to tell. I remember one that used to make me scream. She said that two elderly aristocratic ladies she worked for were sitting one day discussing the size of their you-know-whats. One said to the other, 'You know, the size of your you-know-what depends on the size of your mouth.' And for the rest of the day the other woman pursed her lips up as tight as possible whenever she spoke.

After finishing with Henry I thought nothing more about boys for a bit. I just enjoyed my days and evenings off and Mary's stories and jokes.

My wages had risen quite a bit by now so Mary and I bought the odd bit of silk and had better teas together and danced at the Palais when we could. And we went on a day-trip to Brighton.

I realised I hardly ever went home now. I suppose that was like any youngster really. I had my own life and though I enjoyed going back, nothing much had changed in the East End except the streets were a bit cleaner and some of the worst slums were going – but kids don't go back, do they? Not so much as they should. And I was so busy and wanted fun on my days off. I was also determined to get a husband I liked, so the old East End had to take a back seat for a bit. Then it happened.

Wednesday came round and I had my evening off. I was an expert now at finishing my work on time even if they gave me extra things to do that, in the past, would have kept me late.

I'd reached the entrance to the park when I saw Henry's friend, John. I thought he must be waiting for Henry. He walked up to me, smiled and said he'd come to walk me to the Round Pond, where I was meeting Mary. So off we went. I could hardly say no, could I?

We had a long friendly chat along the way and then, when I spotted Mary in the distance about 20 minutes later, he just touched his hat, turned round and was gone. I think I liked him from the first because he was tactful as well as polite. He talked quietly and listened to what I had to say which was unusual in a man in those days. As he left me and walked off into the trees, I thought, 'That's a pity.'

A week later he was there again, and when he was there the following week I thought something must be up – he's taken a shine to me. I must have liked him a lot because within a few weeks I dreaded reaching the park and finding he hadn't turned up. It would have been like that boy at the Palais all over again.

I used to get so excited hours before I was let off my work and I'd be in a filthy mood if I was given extra jobs to do. John never complained if I was late and he was always there with a big smile. I was in love.

I knew it because I got so fed up with him *not* kissing me that eventually while we walked across the park I asked him straight out why he hadn't kissed me.

'You didn't ask,' he said.

'I'm asking now,' I replied.

So he gave me one of those special kisses. Not a rough desperate kiss but one of those soft lingering ones. I felt a right old trollop because I loved it and kept going back for more. Eventually we stood there kissing for so long that I was really late for Mary. I felt guilty because it was as if I had suddenly changed and moved on. I knew she would sense it. I was leaving her behind.

John had dark hair and was very slim in those days. In fact he never really put much weight on as he grew older because like most men he smoked so much. He always had a fag hanging out of his mouth but I thought it looked very stylish and I loved the smell of tobacco. All that rubbish about smelling like an ashtray. John never smelled like an ashtray. He just had a lovely smell of tobacco about him. I'd always liked the smell of cigarette smoke. I couldn't help it and it was much better than the pipe my mum used to smoke now and then.

Talking of smoking, it always amazed people when I told them my mother smoked a pipe. I don't know where she got her tobacco – probably from the stuff nicked down at the docks, but it smelled like tar. Lots of women smoked pipes in the East End then. Old Irish ladies were the worst – they'd smoke bloody anything. Or they'd mix the tobacco with dried dandelion to make it go a bit further.

I remember telling John how my mum smoked a short stubby clay pipe and he laughed his head off and offered to buy her some cigarettes.

He smoked expensive ones — Capstans they were. They stopped making them eventually as they were murder for the lungs, but even after John died in the 1960s whenever I caught a whiff of tobacco it took me back to those early days when first we met.

Right from the start I knew he was a decent sort; firstly, because he didn't stick his hand up my skirt the first time I kissed him and second he liked dancing. I could never have loved someone who didn't like the Palais. Third, he talked almost straight away about getting married and getting a place of our own. Imagine what that was like for me who'd always lived in tiny bare rooms at the top of cold houses!

John was the first person to call me a communist, but he wasn't being rude. Back in the late 1930s just before the war, being a communist was a good thing. We still thought it meant everyone would be looked after and the toffs wouldn't keep all the best stuff for themselves as they had always done in the past. John and I used to sit in the park talking about revolution. Makes me laugh now when I think of it, but no one knew then what was really happening in Russia.

We just thought it would be great to see some of the lazy good-for-nothings we worked for trying to learn to wash down a step or black a grate. We knew they'd be useless at it, but it would give them a taste of the servants' wasted lives.

But our communist ideas were just pipe dreams. I think we knew it at the time but they brought us together.

John was also the first person I ever heard say that the oppression of the workers wasn't half as bad as the oppression of women. He was a very unusual man in lots of ways.

He had started work in a big house near Berkhamsted in Hertfordshire aged just seven. His dad was a farm labourer and John used to say that his dad thought school, even elementary school, was for the gentry. He used to say to John, 'No point in learning to use your head when you've got to use your hands.' So although he went to school because the law said he had to,

John worked early mornings and Saturdays in the big local house. He used to clean shoes and run errands. The day he left school at 12 years old he started full time.

'I was really upset,' he used to say to me, 'because I loved school and especially reading and I was good at it. But when Dad said hop you hopped.'

By the time I met him John was a right flippin' militant and although most servants were starting to complain about how they were treated, he was much more serious about it. If it hadn't meant the sack he'd have been on marches and protests.

Instead he used to read as much political stuff as he could and he was the only servant I ever met who spent his wages on books. I thought he was mad!

When he started full-time work on the estate, his employers quickly realised he was intelligent. He quickly went from garden boy to footman even though he was a bit short. They liked you to be six foot tall but John made up for his lack of height by being really good looking. He was a really pretty boy, as I used to say to tease him.

We used to joke about being the West End branch of the Communist Party. I was member number one and he was member number two. 'We're small but we're powerful,' he used to say. We were so naïve then. We thought Russia was full of people who didn't have to slave for rich layabouts and who were all equal and got paid and treated well.

'Come the revolution we can eventually all be friends – even the Old Etonian toffs and the farm workers. We'll all be on the production line together.' That's what John used to say. He was too nice really to be a revolutionary. He didn't want to string them up from the nearest lamppost which is what some of the real lefties wanted to do back then.

I was very careful about John because if the family I worked for had found out about him I'd either have been sacked or given a warning not to see him again. But we never got caught and that first summer in the park meeting John every week was the best time of my life. He was a great kisser, too. After a few kisses I can tell you I didn't mind when he did stick his hand up my knickers.

So for us life was kissing in the park and talking about the oppression of the workers. I laugh when I look back now but we did take it quite seriously at the time. John had lots of stories about how servants he knew were treated 'like bloody dirt' as he used to put it. Mind you, he was a bit more generous than I was, saying that some of the people he'd worked for had treated him with kindness, sometimes even respect. We agreed that the other servants were often the worst at oppressing the underdog.

'When I started at the bottom,' he used to say, 'I cried because I couldn't go to school any more. And once I was looking a bit sad while doing some work in the kitchen and the cook gave me a terrific slap across the head. "That's for making faces," she said. I never forgot that or the other indignities I had to put up with.'

But like me he'd had enjoyable days. He told me he'd cycled miles across Hertfordshire in his teens – up as far as Oxford and Banbury just after the First World War ended. He said that all the roads were narrow lanes with the trees crowding overhead – even the main roads – and that you might not see a car for hours. He said that in summer there were so many insects in those pre-insecticide days that the hedges used to fizz with an almost deafening noise of insects and birds as he bicycled past. And what really impressed me about John was that he'd been abroad. I can remember that when he told me he'd been to Paris I nearly fainted. I wasn't even sure where it was!

After that big house at Berkhamsted he'd moved to a job as junior footman in London. But, like me, he wanted to get out of domestic service, so we used to have lots of those lovely fantasy conversations about what we'd do when we'd escaped. We always used to call it escape!

I loved his stories about his London house. Like Mary, he used to exaggerate like mad to make me laugh and it always worked. One story that was true – or at least till the end of his life he insisted it was true – was that every few weeks his employer would ask him to 'apologise to the old man'. That meant he had to go into a big bedroom at the back of the house where the family's mad uncle lived. He wasn't really mad, just very eccentric and probably suffering from dementia or something similar. Anyway, John would knock, go in and apologise for treading on the old man's fingers. The old man would nod, John would back out of the room and the butler would give him a shilling. It happened to the other servants too and no one ever found out what it was all about.

Chapter Twenty-Nine

All this time, after I started seeing John I mean, I felt bad about Mary because I gradually saw less of her. She was always really good about it. I used to apologise like mad and we'd have a funny little exchange. If I saw her on my Sunday off I'd say, 'I don't have to see John this Wednesday. I can miss a week. He won't mind. And I miss having a giggle with you.'

Mary would say, 'You bloody liar. Get out of it. You're mad about him and I'm not going to get in the way of all that kissing. It's disgusting!'

But I always knew she was just teasing and when I said I missed her I really meant it. But I was torn between the two of them and I wasn't like a modern girl with long summer holidays and every weekend to laze about and with time for lots of friends and boyfriends. I had so little time off. You can't imagine it now.

Mary came along with John and me a few times when we had a day out but she looked a bit glum for a lot of the time and it didn't really work. I was worried about all this – pulled one way by John and the other by feeling guilty about Mary. The two of them got on all right, but everyone knows a couple and a single girl going out and being friends never works.

By the end of the summer of 1938 I was seeing John one Wednesday evening and Mary the next. John was a bit unhappy about not seeing me more and so, I think, was Mary.

Then one Wednesday evening when I went to meet Mary she didn't appear. It was then I realised I had no way of contacting her because I didn't know where she worked. She had always been evasive when I'd asked and said, 'Oh, one of those tall terraced houses off Kensington High Street.'

The next time I had a Sunday off I told John she must have got muddled and said I'd have to meet her the following Wednesday evening. When the time came I went along to where we usually met and she still didn't turn up. I felt such a fool for never finding out anything about her.

When you're young you think things will just go on forever. Well they don't. On my next full day off I wandered the Kensington streets thinking I might bump into her. John came along and was really good – even after several hours when, of course, we'd had no luck and we'd stopped miserably for tea. A few weeks later I tried a couple of agencies to see if they would tell me if they had her name down or if she'd come in to make an enquiry. But they were so unhelpful and told me all that sort of stuff was highly confidential. They wouldn't tell me a thing. I can remember crying my eyes out but I knew that Mary had felt pushed out by John and had almost certainly changed jobs to get away.

About a month after that I was called into the housekeeper's room and given a letter with a West Country postmark. The housekeeper gave me a funny look, as if housemaids were not supposed to receive letters. I tucked it into my apron and as soon as the morning's cleaning was over went up to my room to read it. It was of course from Mary. I could barely make out her writing – in fact I think she might even have asked someone else to write it. She said she felt she was getting in my way and that she needed a change from London. She'd got a job back in Somerset. She even put in a few jokes about her new employers. She said they were bloody rich and bloody aristocratic but still a bunch of country bumpkins. She said she'd write again. There was no address so I couldn't write back and that was the end of that. I never heard from her again. It was so shocking. I felt very sad about it for such a long time but what could anyone do?

Chapter Thirty

The history books tell you families were close-knit back then and it was true in a way but not if you went into domestic service. And not really if you were poor. With really big families you were pushed out as soon as you could work and lots of people I met only rarely or never saw their parents or their brothers and sisters again once they'd gone away. Two of my brothers died in the war and a sister died from gangrene. I felt I had hardly known them. Mary knew almost nothing about her brothers and sisters. She told me that, as she was the youngest, several of the older ones had already gone to America by the time she was born and she never met them nor ever expected to.

That was the way it was. Anyone nostalgic about the past always seems to think we lived in little cottages surrounded by roses and went to the well to get lovely cool clean spring water and then spent the morning milking cows as the sun shone. It was never like that in the countryside, according to Mary anyway, and it certainly wasn't like that in Hoxton.

Mary told me it was far worse growing up in the countryside if you had no money. At least there was life in London and you could do things for nothing, even if it was just flirting with the soldiers in the park. She knew girls who went to the local village maybe twice a year for a walk round and the rest of their time was spent working round the farmyard or staring out the window at the rain. At least we had the dance halls, the music hall now and then, and just walking through the crowds in Hoxton.

I only took John home to meet my mum once, which sounds a bit funny but growing up in a cramped, noisy, dirty little place meant we didn't sit around much sipping tea and discussing world affairs. It was all much more chaotic. My mum was nice to John and we had a cup of tea before we legged it. I might have gone back more if we'd had kids later, but we never did.

In those days if you didn't have them you never dreamed of going to the doctor to find out if anything was wrong. Doctors knew very little back then and had a terrible reputation – well, they did in the East End. We thought they'd either make you worse or they'd take your money, rip you off, and then make you worse.

If we didn't have any children it wasn't for lack of trying. We were very daring and slept together a few times before we were married and I don't mind saying I thought it was the best thing I'd ever tried! I thought it was wonderful and, once we were married, we were like a couple of bloody rabbits! John used to say, 'That's why the church doesn't like you having sex unless you intend to have babies. You're not supposed to enjoy life and if you do it means you're an animal. Well I'm an animal and I'm proud of it.'

Growing up in the crowded East End gave you a completely different view of life. You weren't prudish or religious or picky. You didn't have airs and graces because you couldn't be or have any of those things. And though people loved their children – well, mostly they did – anyone who didn't have children was always envied. Always. So John and I never felt the lack of children. He'd grown up in a poor place and so had I, so we knew that if children started to come along they'd never bloomin' stop till we were in the workhouse. So we thought we were lucky. I can honestly say I never regretted it for a minute and no one who'd grown up in the sort of place I grew up in would have thought it was bad luck not to have a brood. John and I had fun together and the fun lasted for much longer than it would have otherwise.

But I'm getting ahead of myself.

I didn't tell the housekeeper at work that I was seeing John and that we'd agreed to get married because I knew I'd be out on my ear the next day. If you got engaged you weren't allowed to work. It was as simple as that. But I'd long ago learned my lesson and I was a sly boots. I wasn't going to let anyone know until it suited me. In fact John and I were really good at keeping our little secret.

I'd been saving for years, and John decided that we'd leave our employers at the same time. We'd get a flat in Islington which was dead cheap then and John would get a job in a factory. We used to talk about our plans for hours in the park and they were such happy days. We were happy later on but more cosy than excited all the time and much as you might love each other into middle and then old age it is never the same as it is at the start. I can still remember how hard it was to get through the days between seeing John each time. I had to wait so long and I was so distracted that I made lots of mistakes. But did I care? Not a bit.

The head housemaid, who was usually nice enough to me, started to get snappy and I got a few lectures. 'How will you ever be promoted to first housemaid if you don't concentrate?' she used to say when, instead of devoting my energies to the carpet fringe, I was staring out the window.

I used to think, 'You must be joking! Who wants a stupid job sweeping up other people's mess for the rest of their lives? Being on top of the dung heap by being head housemaid didn't seem any better to me than being half way up and I thought, 'Yes miss, you keep your dung heap – I'm off out of it!'

We were married in Fulham Register Office on our day off just a few weeks before we both stopped work forever as domestic servants. We had our wedding breakfast in a cafe on Fulham Broadway. There were no guests because we were a right pair of revolutionaries. We didn't really want to get married at all, but John said we'd have trouble with renting places and all sorts of things if we didn't have a marriage certificate and he was probably right. If you weren't married and were known to be living with someone the neighbours could make your life hell.

John always used to say that every youngster has one big thing he or she is brave enough to do – go to Australia, join the army, get out of a terrible job. So that's what we did – we got out of a terrible job. I gave a week's notice and was shocked when the housekeeper begged me to stay. I think she thought I'd be flattered by all the praise she heaped on me. I didn't want to sulk or give her a mouthful because none of it was her fault and she wasn't a bad old stick really. She only gave up when I told her I was already wed. This was 1939 and she knew that by now it was a lot harder to get good servants. What she didn't know was that the war, when it came, was going to make things a lot worse and many little old ladies who thought they were too refined to do anything for themselves were soon going to be either eating beans out of tins or learning to open and close the oven door!

Chapter Thirty-One

After the Second World War most of the middle classes who'd had servants had reduced their staff to one or two at most and upped their wages. And what amazed me most of all was that I heard employers had become more polite. It was, 'Would you mind helping me with this?' and 'Do you think you could manage lunch for 1.00 pm?'

What really made me smile was when I accidentally bumped into someone who had been a housemaid with me in the early 1930s. This would have been in the 1950s. She told me that the family she worked for treated her like gold dust, they were so scared she'd leave. If she asked for two weeks' paid holiday they gave it to her without a murmur. She told me she nearly fainted one day when she saw the master throw a log on the fire himself. That was a real sign of how much things had changed after I left. A bit of me thought, 'Bloody typical. I work all those years at the worst time and as soon as I leave it all gets better and servants get treated by their employers as if they were best friends.'

It must still have been tough, though, because you could never escape that English thing of not quite being one of them, if you see what I mean.

But John and I were as free as birds. We set up in a nice little flat in Islington just off the Essex Road and we were very happy. It's much easier to be happy in a marriage if you've both had a tough time before you get married. It's as if you've been rescued – by each other. You don't sit around thinking that if you were with someone else or had loads more money or a house in France you'd be happier. You concentrate on where you've come from much more and John and I always thought we'd lived at a lucky time; a time when there was well-paid work away from the drudgery of service. John's dad and granddad had never left the estates where they'd worked. They'd lived and died in service, but we'd got away. Things were on the up.

I had a few jobs after the war and John did well working with his brother as an odd-job man. A bit of carpentry, a bit of gardening and even bricklaying. He gave up the factory idea. You see, London had to be re-built and John helped with a lot of it – well, that's what I like to think. It wasn't well-paid work but work was always there and he loved being with his brother. They worked all over the place and they were independent.

I had a job for a few months on a stall in Chapel Street market in Islington. That was a laugh. I got the job through a friend and I used to stand there shouting, 'Edwards! Pound a tanner!' meaning a pound of King Edwards potatoes for sixpence. After all those years of being quiet while I worked I could bellow at the top of my voice – I loved it. That and the banter between the costers and other stall holders. I left that job because you had to be up so early and in winter that was no joke. My days of getting up early were over!

Chapter Thirty-Two

But there you are, you see. I left as soon as I wanted to because I could.

We never bought our little flat. Most people of my social class and age were too scared to make a big commitment like that. We didn't even have bank accounts, so we could never have had a mortgage. We didn't even dare go in a bank. One look at us or an earful of us speaking and they'd think we were bank robbers! I finally got a bank account in the late 1970s long after John was dead and I remember thinking, 'Blimey, I've finally arrived.'

But I never really got the hang of how a bit of signed paper was the same as a one-pound note. But we all get out of date and it's no bad thing because the real work in every new world is for the youngsters. We're not supposed to try to do what they do or we'll spoil it for them. They like us old people being out of touch and not trying to keep up. I never really got the hang of decimalisation either but the best thing that ever happened to me was the television and getting into an old people's home. In an old people's home they leave the heating on all the time. You get a bed soft enough for a princess and people bring you tea in the mornings and lunch at one. I can have it in my room or in the dining room. It's like everything has come round full circle. I'm the one that gets waited on now. But I hope I'm always nice to the staff. We have a laugh, although they must get fed up with all us old girls babbling on about the past. Well, we have to don't we, because we only have the past? That's where we live most of the time.

Chapter Thirty-Three

That whole world I knew has gone as if it never existed. It always makes me laugh when I try to think of the biggest difference between then and now. It's not the way we were treated or the vanished horses or the drab clothes. No. I'd say the biggest difference between then and now was that we were all so bloomin' awful smelly! It wasn't the lack of bathrooms (though we never had one) or all sleeping in one or two rooms; it was the fact that there wasn't any deodorant! And even if there had been we couldn't have paid for it!

Sounds a bit wicked I know, but though I'm not sad about the past being gone, I do miss the time when Stepney and Whitechapel were almost no go areas for the police. We didn't care a damn for the authorities so long as we didn't get nicked; we'd do what we liked. Any toff down the East End in my mum's day would be lucky to get out alive, and serve 'em right. They were on our territory.